HIDDEN TREASURES

TREASURES

How to Realize Your Potential

Based on the Kabbalah
and the teachings of
REBBE NACHMAN OF BRESLOV

by
Chaim Kramer

with
Yitzchok Bell

Published by
Breslov Research Institute
Jerusalem/New York

This edition has been dedicated by

Yosef Yaakov Ben-Zev

may he and his family live and be well
wife Rochel Leah and children Eliyahu Leib,
Ephraim Aharon, Tzvi Dov, Shmaya YomTov,
Esther Shayna and Chaim Pinchas

in honor of

Rosh Kollel Chatzos Breslov in Beitar Illit
Rabbi Yehoshua Meir Deutsch, *shlita*

who has merited to promote and proliferate the
unique mitzvah of "*Chatzos*" throughout the world,
and to spread the name of Rebbe Nachman in
Eretz Yisrael and across the globe.

It is also dedicated in honor of the eminent Kollel
Chatzos scholars who rise from sleep to "stand in
Hashem's house at night" — to study in the exalted
and awesome hours when all the gates of heaven
are open, and all prayers are accepted, and blessing
and salvation are drawn into the world. As the holy
Zohar states: All those who merit waking up and
studying Torah at this auspicious time have "a thread
of lovingkindness drawn over them," and all the
blessings bestowed upon them will be fulfilled.

Table of Contents

Foreword

Rebbe Nachman once said: "I will take you on a new path—a path that has never before existed. It is indeed an ancient path. Yet it is completely new" *(Tzaddik #264).*

The path that Rebbe Nachman revealed to his followers at the turn of the nineteenth century is just as applicable—if not more so—to those of us living in the twenty-first century. Now as then, people are confronted with so many challenges and obstacles to living the kind of life they desire. We all struggle to earn a living, marry and have children, maintain relationships, and find avenues of self-fulfillment rather than live out our days with a sense of futility. We desire to be active participants in our life's journey, not passive observers.

Rebbe Nachman also put his finger on the pulse of the times by saying, "I will tell you a secret. Great atheism is coming into the world."

Two hundred years later, we understand exactly what Rebbe Nachman was talking about. We now know that this atheism doesn't just mean the abandonment of God and religion, but estrangement from our own selves. Rebbe Nachman addressed an age when feelings of emptiness would predominate, while at the same time, longing and yearning to change and accomplish would surge within each individual. He developed his teachings to meet the needs of every seeker, as well as the noncommittal onlooker who doubts his own ability to succeed. The Rebbe's doctrine is one of joy and hope, his approach common sense, as he encourages each of us to set our sights higher and higher.

What made Rebbe Nachman different from many other Chassidic masters was his ability to access the mysteries of the Kabbalah and extract practical advice for living one's life to the fullest. Beginning with one of the first secrets of Creation—how God went about creating the world as we know it—Rebbe Nachman drew out the practical lessons of each stage of Creation and the Ten Sefirot and laid them out on a "set table" for each of us to view, select and sample. By bringing the most esoteric concepts down to our level, Rebbe Nachman left us an awesome legacy that can help us overcome the atheism in our world and in our own souls.

This book holds out two tantalizing opportunities to the modern-day reader. The first is to *realize* or recognize the tremendous resources and strengths that are uniquely yours. Each person is a world unto himself, possessing unique attributes and capabilities as well as characteristic weaknesses and vulnerabilities. Only by knowing yourself can you identify and pursue your dearest objectives, and ignore what is beyond you or not applicable to your life. The second is to attain your *potential* by learning how to develop your hidden strengths to the optimum, becoming the person you would love to be, the person you can—and should—be.

Hidden Treasures is not a general guide to Kabbalah, nor a mass-market commentary explaining how the Kabbalistic system works. It is a learning experience, a guide for applying the deepest mysteries of existence to our seemingly mundane lives. It applies to laymen and scholars, religious and nonobservant, men and women. It shows how great and important we are in God's eyes, and how we can develop that greatness. It tells us how we can take hold of our energies even during moments of crisis, and advance from level to level, growing even—or especially—in the face of adversity. *Hidden Treasures* will take you beyond your perceived limits and propel you to unimagined heights.

* * *

I wish to express my thanks to my dear friend, Yitzchok Bell, who made use of all his innermost energies and powers of persuasion to "force" me to undertake this work. His compilation and organization of the teachings of Rebbe Nachman as they apply to each Sefirah brought this book into existence in the first place. To Y. Hall, our editor who brooked "no excuses" in making me "realize the potential" of this book, challenging me at every step to do better. To our staff at Breslov Research Institute, who put up with me through the long and frustrating days and nights. And above all, to my wife, whose patience and endurance win her the prize for living through the most potentially problematic provocations, yet remaining faithful through it all.

Chaim Kramer
Adar 5767/March 2007

Part One

REALIZE YOUR
POTENTIAL

1
THE POWER OF POTENTIAL

Everyone has potential. Enormous potential. When we develop our potential, we can transform it into great deeds and accomplishments. We can live a life of contentment. Our days will be filled with substance. Work, leisure time and all our daily routines can take on meaningful expression.

What exactly is our potential? More importantly, how can we develop it?

Potential is a unique energy granted to each and every person by God Himself, and it resides within each person's unique soul. We can better understand this idea from the verse *(Genesis* 2:7), "And He breathed into him a breath of life." That is, when God breathed into Adam his soul, He was breathing into man His limitless power and energy. As the noted Kabbalist, the ARI (1534-1572), explains, "When God exhales, He 'exhales' from His innermost being. Furthermore, once this breath is breathed into man, it cannot be severed from Him" *(Etz Chaim*, p. 68; see *Innerspace*, p. 17; *Anatomy of the Soul*, pp. 30-31). Thus, man is a vessel that contains God's breath of life, and he retains a direct connection to the Infinite God. As a vessel, he can definitely reflect that "breath"—that is, the energy it contains. In this way, man is a personal repository of enormous, near-infinite potential.

The reason we are not fully aware of our potential is due to its depth. Our potential is linked directly to God, but like God, Who is not readily apparent, our potential also is not readily apparent. Were we only to look inward to evaluate what strengths we possess, and review our lives to see where we've come from and how we accomplished what we did until now, we could begin to recognize a bit of that potential.

Everything in creation displays the same depth. For example, scientists first discovered the atom, then the neutron, then quantum, etc. The discovery of each layer led to an additional search for deeper and more energy-charged particles within the atom. Similarly, untold layers envelop a person's innermost being. Each level that is revealed and activated sets the stage for the next level to be attained.

Usually people don't really know what their potential is or how powerful it can be until they are faced with a challenge. Then they somehow discover enormous strengths or resources with which to confront and conquer difficult or even impossible situations. People undertake daring rescue efforts or act in completely uncharacteristic ways when put to the test. At those moments, they are tapping those awesome reservoirs of energy stored deep within that allow them to accomplish so many things—even those that seem beyond their capabilities.

Wouldn't it be nice if we didn't have to wait for a challenge to unlock the mystery of our potential? Wouldn't it be better to access it at will? Imagine how much satisfaction we could gain by harnessing its unbelievable power.

We can—using the tools of the Kabbalah.

2

THE TOOLS

Knowing that we have potential is one thing. Being able to develop it is the next step. Just as precious metals like gold and diamonds must be extracted from the earth with specialized tools, we need proper tools to "mine" our depths in order to develop our potential. What are those tools?

In the biblical account of Creation, we find that God created man and placed him on this earth. Since God intended that we become responsible human beings, we must assume that God gave us the tools with which to develop ourselves. He did: He gave us both a soul and a body, the ability to develop our thoughts and to turn them into actuality. Used in tandem, the body and the soul are the tools we need to survive—and succeed—in this world.

God gave us a third gift—the benefit of His Wisdom and guidance. Through His Torah, He teaches us to grow, mature and attain unparalleled heights, both emotionally and spiritually. Only through the Torah, whose teachings are explained and embellished in the prism of the Kabbalah and Chassidut, can we understand the power we possess and the best way to develop our unique potential.

What is the Torah?

The Torah is the document received by the Jewish People at Mount Sinai and transmitted in its entirety by Moses some 3,300 years ago, along with the Oral Tradition that accompanied that document. This Oral Torah elucidates the basic meaning of the Written Torah (an extremely terse text that contains much more than it reveals) and explains how to fulfill its commandments. God gave both the Written and Oral Torahs at Sinai. Today the Written Torah is known as the Five Books of Moses and the Oral Torah is known as the Mishnah, Talmud, Midrash, the Kabbalah and related texts.

The Oral Torah dovetails with the Written Torah in four primary ways, identified by the Hebrew acronym, *Pardes*. (*Pardes* is the source for the English word *Paradise*, which refers to the Garden of Eden.) *PaRDeS* refers to the four different levels of understanding the Torah: *Pshat* (simple meaning), *Remez* (allusion), *Drush* (moral lessons) and *Sod* (secret meaning, Kabbalah). Taken together, these four levels are the keys needed to enter the Paradise of the Torah.

With these four keys, the Torah opens up and reveals not only its own secrets, but the secrets of the universe—the secrets of matter (space), history (time) and man (soul and consciousness). If we wish to probe the mysteries of Creation and human existence, the Torah is the address. This is the document which God created before He created the world, and which He used as His "blueprint" for Creation. The Torah is nothing less than an illumination of what we call God's Mind. It is the conceptual link between Him and His world, between Him and us.

Generally, when we speak of Torah, we think of it as the "body" of laws spelled out in the Written and Oral Torahs. This reflects our understanding that the Torah is a structure of ideas that we can relate to, a distinct form that stands out as the Halakhah, the legal system of Torah. But as a body of laws, Halakhah sometimes seems to lack that inner dimension that motivates us to observe it, as witnessed by the many who feel alienated from its study and practice. Looking only at the body of Torah, one fails to recognize its inner soul, the depths that lie beneath the surface. This is where the Kabbalah comes into play.

The Kabbalah

In a remarkably short time, a tremendous thirst for spirituality has taken hold of the world. In a sense, the vast material wealth and comforts with which we have been blessed are now accompanied by a gnawing lack of fulfillment. Material benefits satisfy, but they don't last very long. If we eat, we must eat again soon. Sensual pleasures bring a certain amount of gratification, but evoke additional wants. Everyone feels some longing, some yearning, some lack. "How can I experience a long-lasting contentment, one that stays with me, one that is engraved on my inner being?" people ask. It is this emotional hunger that has led many to search in earnest for their connection to God and Godliness.

To meet the demand, a plethora of books have flooded the market, among them works purporting to explain the Kabbalah as the major means to attach oneself to the Divine. Whether the pursuit of God is another passing fad or a truly serious quest remains to be seen. Yet one wonders: What has made the Kabbalah the popular handbook of seekers? What exactly *is* the Kabbalah?

The Hebrew word *kabbalah* means received. It designates a body of knowledge that has been received prophetically and transmitted faithfully from generation to generation.

One of the basic tenets of the Kabbalah is that everything that exists in the physical dimension has a parallel in the spiritual dimension. (Indeed, one of the cognates of the word *KaBbaLaH* is *haK'BaLaH*, meaning parallelism or correspondence.) This follows the ancient Kabbalistic teaching: "As above, so below; as below, so above."

In order to grasp this principle, the initial stage of Kabbalah study is usually devoted to mastering its complex system of correspondences. These correspondences are in no way to be thought of as mechanical. Rather, they afford an inside view of the interrelationships that govern all existence, and lead us back to the root and source of all complexity—the Infinite Being Himself, Who created and continues to sustain the entire multidimensional hologram we call "The Universe."

In order to "think Kabbalah," we must also acknowledge its integral part in our daily lives. For example, everything in creation, mankind included, possesses a dual nature. We can readily see that the human body is comprised of many intricate and interconnected organs, joints, sinews, veins, etc. Yet as complex as the body is, it is just a form. It lacks the ability to do anything by itself unless directed by a deeper dimension—i.e., the soul. Under the soul's direction, all the intricate body parts play their role to act out a person's desires and allow him to attain his goal. On the other hand, having a deeper dimension but lacking the form that would bring that depth into an actual structure, leaves everything in a state of suspended animation. There is no goal, for there is no form.

In the same way that the soul animates the body, the Kabbalah enlivens the Torah. As mentioned above, the Torah is the document received and transmitted by Moses. Of the four keys to understanding the Torah, the first three—the simple meaning, the allusive meaning and the moral lessons—are basically related to the "body" of Torah, the form. This body, like the human body, requires a soul to set it in motion. The Kabbalah is that "soul," the deep mysteries that unlock the innermost secrets of the Torah. Like the soul of a person, the Kabbalah provides the attraction and motivation that move a person to seek God. By extension, the Kabbalah also contains the necessary mystique to motivate a person to develop his potential, to seek and search even deeper into life and its meaning.

Accessing the Kabbalah

Notwithstanding the power of the Kabbalah, which contains the mysteries of Creation—indeed, of life itself—how can the average person find the answers he seeks in its study?

Even a superficial study of the Kabbalah shows that most of its texts speak of God's Names and their corresponding applications. Since the Kabbalah is meant to reveal that God is everywhere, it makes sense that everything will be a parallel to God and Godliness. However, the vast majority of people do not understand these parallelisms, especially in the Kabbalah's protracted texts. And even if we did have some knowledge of the mystery of God's presence, how would that help us *apply* that knowledge to our daily lives?

This question is important, as it reflects a fundamental Kabbalistic teaching. When God created man, He gave him the power of free choice to do good or evil. When man performs a good deed, he enables God's Light to shine down on this material world. When he does an evil deed, he causes an obstruction of God's Light. Ironically, the further one distances himself from God, the greater the revelation of Godliness one needs to return to Him. A strenuous jump might lift a person a few feet off the ground, but only sophisticated rocket power can elevate man from the Earth to the stratosphere. So too, one who is distant from God requires a much greater revelation of Him (i.e., a more powerful energy than is usually available) to make the leap from his material quagmire to spiritual freedom.

In earlier generations, people of great stature—prophets, sages and those of pure souls—were well-versed in the Written and Oral Torahs. It was sufficient for them to experience God with heightened awareness, without resorting to the depths of the Kabbalah. In those days, the Kabbalistic system was reserved for a few "initiates" who were allowed to delve into its mysteries, as we find in the Talmud (*Chagigah* 11b-14b) and the Zohar.

In subsequent generations, however, people began to grow very distant from God and sank to unparalleled levels of debasement. As the generations regressed more and more, they lost their attachment to the higher, Supernal Worlds. Now the only energy that can truly reach out to us in these difficult times is found in the teachings of the Kabbalah. It is the level of Keter, the highest and ineffable level, which still illuminates the darkest places and sustains each and every individual (see p. 59). It is specifically that level which reaches down to us and gives us sustenance and nourishment.

Rebbe Nachman teaches:

> Know! The Torah enclothed in the deepest concealments is specifically elevated Torah [i.e., the Kabbalah], which is the energy God uses to sustain the lower worlds. It is this energy which is found in lowly places—within those who have sinned so extensively that God is so totally hidden from them. ... This corresponds to (Exodus 12:12 and Passover Haggadah), "I will pass through the land of Egypt on that night—I, and not an angel... I, and not a messenger—for I am God, I, and no other." In the land of Egypt, where the concealment was very great, Israel was submerged in Forty-Nine Gates of Impurity, and so, specifically there, God Himself is enclothed and concealed (Likutey Moharan I, 56:4).

Keter is also the level that provides the answers to life's mysteries. It provides the necessary advice to develop our potential so that we can face up to and cope with life's challenges.

But how can we, who are most in need of the Kabbalah's teachings, access and comprehend its hidden depths?

In a stunning reversal of history, the knowledge of the Kabbalah that was once reserved for a select group of "initiates" was slowly revealed to more and more people until the Baal Shem Tov, founder of Chassidism, and his great-grandson, Rebbe Nachman of Breslov, made those teachings not only accessible but applicable to all.

The decision to reveal the Kabbalah to the masses was not an easy one. Until the destruction of the Second Holy Temple in 68 C.E.—and in the years immediately following that national cataclysm—knowledge of the Kabbalah was tightly restricted due to the fear that its insights and continuous usage of God's Holy Names would encourage unworthy people to perform miracles by invoking those Names, leading an already subdued nation in exile further astray. This fear was validated by the Zohar itself, which teaches that the main reason for the long exile and its oppressive suffering is because Torah mysteries are disclosed to the unworthy (*Tikkuney Zohar* #56, p. 90a; cf. *Zohar* III, 128a).

But as the pressures of the exile mounted steadily—the oppression of the Church, the birth of Islam, the rise of the Karaite sects and other distortions of Torah and authentic Judaism—the Kabbalists finally decided to expand their circles. This expansion was originally intended for small groups of initiates, but it burgeoned rapidly after the Church established the Inquisition during the fifteenth century.

With the advent of the ARI in the sixteenth century, the Kabbalah began to spread further afield. Many Halakhic authorities, recognizing the import of these teachings and their impact upon the common folk, began to incorporate Kabbalistic teachings in their decisions. This was especially true in the period following the Chmelnicki massacres (1648-1649), which began in eastern Ukraine and spread across Europe, leaving nearly a million Jews dead and thousands of Jewish communities in ruins. The masses sought hope and salvation amidst the ruins, and were open to anything that might lift them out of their despair.

Unfortunately, the fears of those who wished to contain the Kabbalah because of the unworthy who would abuse its power were realized at that time. A charismatic Jewish preacher named Shabbetai Zvi began to espouse the Kabbalah in 1666, using it as a basis for his heretical interpretation of himself as the long-awaited Messiah. He misled many thousands of people—among them rabbinical leaders of the generation—and was single-handedly responsible for the destruction of hundreds of Jewish communities around the world which followed him into apostasy. Shabbateanism continued well into the eighteenth century, eating away at the basis of faith and distancing myriads of Jews from their roots.

In the aftermath of the Shabbetai Zvi affair, the Kabbalah again became the focus of heated discussion: "Should it be revealed…?" "But we need it to sustain us…?" As these discussions turned into debates, and the debates degenerated into outright battles, the Baal Shem Tov appeared on the scene.

Chassidut

Born in Ukraine in 1698, the Baal Shem Tov strove for and attained incredible heights of spirituality. His understanding was so keen that he could bring the most esoteric teachings about God down to the level of the most ignorant of people. He expounded upon the centrality of man in creation and how God holds everyone in great esteem. God is *always* connected to man (see above, p. 11). However, it is up to man to develop that connection and make it solid. (See *This Land is My Land*, Part VI, for an in-depth review of the revelation of the Kabbalah during the eighteenth century.)

The Baal Shem Tov was well aware of the hidden mysteries of the Torah and could tap into their energy. He took the deepest mysteries of the Torah and explained them in a manner that revealed the Torah for what it was meant to be—a guide for survival and life in this world.[1] The Baal Shem Tov founded the Chassidic movement which, from its inception, was able to inspire even the lowliest person with a real and deep-rooted feeling of Godliness.

Not only did the Baal Shem Tov excel in his transmission of Torah, he was able to infuse his leading followers—themselves great Kabbalists and righteous men—with the same ability to transmit that hidden message so that others could avail themselves of the secret energy of Keter. Keter parallels the level of *Atika Stimaah* (the Ancient Concealed One), from whence emanates the Torah to be revealed in the time of the Mashiach. The Mashiach himself is called *Pele Yo'eitz* (Wondrous Advisor), reflecting the fact that the Kabbalah and the hidden levels of Torah contain the counsel we need to face the challenges of life and overcome them.

The world of the Kabbalah is unique in that of all the Torah texts we can study, the Kabbalistic teachings are the ones that touch the heart most profoundly. Even a cursory study of Chassidic writings delivers teachings that resonate and inspire as they expound on life's mysteries in a most practical manner. "This is something I

---

[1] The Hebrew word *ToRaH* shares the same root as the word *ToReH* (to teach or guide).

can relate to!" and, "This was said specifically for me!" are some of the oft-quoted reactions after a session of Chassidic study. All the Chassidic masters developed their own unique style to eloquently transmit these teachings to those who earnestly searched for the Godliness in everything.

Rebbe Nachman of Breslov

Of all the great Chassidic luminaries, no one was better able to master this ability of turning the esoteric into the simple than Rebbe Nachman of Breslov (1772-1810). A great-grandson of the Baal Shem Tov, Rebbe Nachman's brilliance in transmitting the Divine message that emanates from the Kabbalah can be seen in page after page, paragraph after paragraph, and line after line of his writings. The whole of Torah translates into eminently practical and personal advice in his teachings, which were transcribed and disseminated by his main disciple, Reb Noson of Breslov.

This book invites you to takes those hidden mysteries of Torah, revealed to us in the esoteric form of the Kabbalah, and turn them into guideposts for developing your capabilities and experiencing life as it should be lived—to its fullest. With Rebbe Nachman as our guide, let us tap into the secret mysteries of the Torah to reveal the wisdom of the Kabbalah in its most exalted form—that of practical advice.

.

Part Two

IN THE BEGINNING

1

FIRST THOUGHT

To understand the inner workings of the universe and tap into their awesome power, we must go back to the beginning, to Creation. The Torah, which starts "in the beginning," is our authoritative guide to what happened during the Seven Days of Creation. What happened *before* Creation—namely, how God approached this new project and His intentions for it—falls under the purview of the Kabbalah.

The stories we read in the Torah are not just pages out of history. They are meant to be a guide to each and every one of us as we live our own lives. Scripture states (*Genesis* 5:1), "This is the book of the chronicles of *Adam* (man)." Reb Noson explains this verse to mean, "These accounts are the chronicles of each and every person." Every person can find direction for himself and his goals if he but looks into the Torah and fathoms its depths to interpret its meaning on a personal level (see *Likutey Halakhot, Nesiat Kapayim* 5:27).

In the same way, the Kabbalistic teachings of how the world came into existence illuminate the way in which we too can bring our goals to fruition. The Kabbalah's description of God's "step-by-step" approach to creating the world, as well as all the Supernal Universes that preceded it, does not depict an arbitrary process.

Through Creation, God developed a spiritual blueprint that applies not only to forming new worlds but also to choosing a career or undertaking a difficult project. The very first step in God's plan, as in our own, is the "first thought."

Rabbi Shlomo Alkabetz, a leading sixteenth-century Kabbalist, composed the *Lekha Dodi* hymn which is sung in all congregations during Friday-night services. In this hymn he wrote, "Last in deed is first in thought." Ostensibly, this refers to the creation of the Sabbath, the final day and goal of the first six days of Creation. But it also applies to the way we should approach any goal. Our potential to accomplish lies within our own individual thoughts. We must learn how to react to our thoughts and focus on them, using our creative abilities to grasp the dimensions of our ideas and build the necessary parameters, so that these "first thoughts" can develop into real deeds.

To illustrate how this works, Rebbe Nachman gives the example of someone who wants to build a house. At first the builder must imagine what the house will look like, where it will be built, and the time frame of its construction. After drawing up the blueprints, selecting the location and resolving the time elements, he will purchase the property and materials and go to work. The final deed of completing the house was actually in his first thought, for he imagined its construction down to the last detail. Thus, "Last in deed (the finished house) is first in thought"—that first thought contained everything *in potentia*.

Thinking, creative human beings are the goal of Creation. Rebbe Nachman repeatedly told his followers that no two people are—nor ever were, nor ever will be—exactly alike. Each and every one of us has unusual qualities that allow our originality to develop. Rebbe Nachman's message is clear: People are not clones, and trying to be "like others" automatically inhibits creativity. We must focus on our *own* individual strengths and perfect them. Only then can we fully develop our potential.

With these ideas in mind, let us now examine exactly how God created the world, and the messages He wished to convey to us.

2

❦

THE TZIMTZUM

Before we expound on the following principles of the Kabbalah, we must recall the most important advisory issued by the Kabbalists: We must never attribute any physical form or shape either to God or to the spiritual worlds. All the anthropomorphic terminology mentioned in the Kabbalah is only employed to bring profound concepts down to a level that we can understand. Thus, we will be illustrating the Creation using figurative terms like "anger," "patience," "love," "joy," "right hand," "left hand," "body," "mind," etc. The application of these patently human terms of emotion and form do not apply literally to the Divine.

When God first conceived the Creation, the entire universe came into being both "potentially" and "actually." Since God is not subject to the rules of form, space or time (which He Himself created), when God "thinks" of something, the potential and the actual are always one. The difference between them is only seen from our perspective. Moreover, because we are bound by form, space and time, we can only conceive of God's thought as being "before" Creation and the manifestation of that thought as being "after" Creation. Therefore, God "had to," as it were, delineate the process of Creation to show us how to use our own creative powers to separate between the two.

Prior to Creation, only God existed. God is known as the *Ein Sof* (The Infinite), and He is everywhere. The concept of infinity is so impossible to grasp that the Kabbalists do not even speak of God as the Ein Sof. Rather, they refer to Him as the *Ohr Ein Sof* (The Light of the Infinite). We can say, though, that with only God in existence, there was no room for anything else to exist simultaneously. How, then, did the world come into being? The ARI describes how Creation took place:

> Before all things were created…the Supernal Light was simple [i.e., complete and perfect]. It filled all existence. There was no empty space which could be characterized as space, emptiness or void. Everything was filled with that simple Ohr Ein Sof. There was no category of beginning and no category of end. All was one simple, undifferentiated, Infinite Light.
>
> When it arose in His Will to create worlds and emanate emanations…He constricted (withdrew) His Infinite Essence away from the very center point of His Light. [Of course, since Infinity has no center point, this is only said from the point of view of the Space that is about to be created.] He then withdrew that Light [even further], distancing it to the extremities around this center point, leaving a Vacated Space and Hollow Void.
>
> After this constriction, which resulted in the creation of a Vacated Space and Hollow Void in the very midst of the Infinite Light, there was a place for all the Four Worlds that were to be emanated (*Atzilut*), created (*Beriyah*), formed (*Yetzirah*) and completed (*Asiyah*). He then drew a single, straight *Kav* (Ray or Line) down from His Infinite Surrounding Light into the Vacated Space. This Kav descended in stages into the Vacated Space. The upper extremity of this Kav touched the Infinite Light [that surrounded the Space], and extended down [into the Vacated Space towards the center] but not all the way to the bottom extremity [so as not to cause the Vacated Space to collapse and merge back into the Infinite Light]. It was through this Kav [serving as a conduit] that the Light of the Infinite was drawn down and spread out below.…Through this

Kav, the outpouring Supernal Light of the Infinite spreads forth and flows down into the universes that are located within that Space and Void (*Etz Chaim, Drush Igulim V'Yosher* 1:2).

Thus, a tiny constriction of Godliness was later expanded into a larger void of Godliness known as the Vacated Space. Only within this Vacated Space could the world come into being. In the language of the Kabbalists, the process of creating this Vacated Space was called the *Tzimtzum*—the "constriction" or "contraction" of Godliness—which God implemented in order to "make room" for the rest of Creation. Only after the Tzimtzum could there be a place for the Creation. Indeed, immediately after the Tzimtzum, God began creating, forming and making all the Supernal Universes, the Ten Sefirot and the Supernal Worlds, culminating in the creation of our physical world.

What is unique to the concept of tzimtzum is that although its energy represents constriction, it is that same energy that allows for creativity to burst forth into actuality, as we shall soon see.

Let us apply the Act of Creation to our personal lives (based on Rebbe Nachman's lesson in *Likutey Moharan* I, 66). As we say in our daily prayers, Creation is enacted every day (cf. "He Who renews Creation every day" [*Morning Prayers*]). Simply put, each day is a *new* day. We all wake up with fresh ideas, new insights, and projects and goals we wish to complete, whether for our family, our career, our emotional needs or our spiritual desires. Each day a person could use his creativity to tackle an old problem from a different angle; ponder a creative way to embark on a new path; start a new diet; rearrange exercise, leisure or sleep habits; begin a new relationship, etc.

Just as the first step in Creation was God's thought to create the world, so too, our first thoughts represent our potential to turn ideas into actuality.[2] However, in the beginning, our thoughts aren't

---

[2] Rebbe Nachman teaches that when one originates a thought that brings him a desire for accomplishment, he has already created a soul "in potential." (The Hebrew word for soul, *nefesh*, also connotes "desire.") To bring that new soul into actuality, one must articulate his desire clearly (*Likutey Moharan* I, 31:6-8).

always focused. We may be overwhelmed by all the things we'd like to accomplish and sense that there's not enough time to do everything. Our thoughts might illumine our minds with a bright light, but they lack clear direction.

We must start by clarifying the form and the temporal and spatial nature of our intended goal. This is why the very next step after the "first thought" is the tzimtzum. In practical terms, this means delineating our plans. Similar to building a house, we must conceive a form, a place and a time frame within which we can shape our intentions into feasible and manageable proportions.

As we begin to develop our thoughts, however, we invariably run up against unexpected problems and obstacles. True, we accept that there will be challenges, and we are sure we can overcome them. But as soon as we actually confront the obstacles, we may begin to question our decisions, find material difficulties (e.g., time, familial or financial constraints), or get bogged down in the details. We can lose patience, become frustrated, and even become unhinged from the "impossibility" of our mission. And we might succumb to anger.

But that is exactly what is supposed to happen (not the anger or unhinging)! In the realm of potential, things seem easy enough. When we buckle down to get the job done, however, things don't go as planned. In reality, these experiences are a natural outcome of our own personal "creation" process. They represent the tzimtzum, those constrictions that are placed upon us as we try to transform our thoughts from potentiality to actuality. We experience feelings of frustration and anger in particular because tzimtzum connotes restraint and can also imply anger.

One reason God created the Tzimtzum was to teach us the proper way to go about developing our potential. The constriction shows us how to separate potential from actual in order to allow the actual to emerge. The separation process is a function unto itself.

Remember that when God thought about creating the world, it was as if the world were already created. For man to exist, however, God, as it were, had to "separate" Himself from the world, so that man would not be overwhelmed by His awesome Light. That separation process is a difficult one (not for Him, but for us), yet is necessary in order to turn potential into actual.

To understand how the separation process fits in with the idea of tzimtzum, we turn to Scripture's description of the Creation (*Isaiah* 48:13): "Even My [left] hand (*af Yadi*) has established the earth, and My right [hand] has measured the Heavens." God formed Heaven and Earth with His "two hands."

Imagine that you are trying to build something with your two hands. If they were joined together, would you be able to build anything? Obviously not. So when God began to create the world, although by Him everything (potential and actual) is joined together, He separated between the potential and the actual to launch the creative process. This is the allusion to God's "right hand" and "left hand." It refers to making a separation and/or an opening between the right and the left, between the potential and the actual.

Rebbe Nachman adds that what God did is alluded to in the beginning of the verse, "*af Yadi*." The Hebrew word *af* also translates as anger, representing the constriction. The constrictions—the anger and the frustrations that we experience—are what give us the energy to move towards our goals and learn how to separate between the potential and the actual.

We can all imagine an idyllic world, though we never seem to get close to it. There is just too much suffering, illness, poverty and crime standing in the way of the most utopian plans. We must make the effort to differentiate between what we truly want and what we can honestly attain. This separation can easily lead a person to frustration or anger over not being able to fulfill his goals—but that would be counterproductive. The constriction—the tzimtzum—

provides a filter to help clarify our thoughts and bring us to face reality: "What is it that I can *really* accomplish?"

The tzimtzum serves to snap us out of our dream world and wake us up to real life. It alerts us to the task at hand, making us cognizant of what is available to us. Its true purpose is to create an atmosphere of tranquility *within us*, to quiet and control the flow of activity around us, and to bring us to an awareness of how much we can achieve when we get down to work.

By extension, the tzimtzum teaches us that the very first characteristics we want to nurture are patience with ourselves and tolerance towards others. When we exercise patience, we can control the constrictions of our lives. "I can't lose thirty pounds in a day. But I can be patient and work on it and lose that weight in a fixed period of time." "I can't save a lot of money on my salary. But I can be patient and put aside a little bit from each paycheck so that after a while it will add up to a substantial sum."

Tolerance is also integral to our goals. There are many people whom we love, whom we want to love, whom we feel indifferent about, and whom we want nothing to do with. Each of those people, in his or her unique way, can pose an obstacle to our goals. We must learn to restrain our anger and generate our own tranquil atmosphere to increase our chances of succeeding.

Certainly, the attribute of patience applies equally, if not more, to pursuing emotional and spiritual growth. A person should focus on these latter goals most of all if he wishes to become someone who is in control of himself.

"In the beginning God created the Heavens and the Earth. And the Earth was without form and desolate, with darkness upon the abyss, [but] the spirit of God hovered upon the waters. And God said, 'Let there be light'" (*Genesis* 1:1-3).

First must come the creativity of our thoughts—the "Heavens"—where our potential lies. Afterwards, we try to turn those thoughts into "Earth"—a usable and productive venue. But first we must face the tzimtzum—the formlessness, desolation, darkness and abyss. We know that we *can* accomplish, since the "spirit of God" hovers upon us and within us, in the form of our souls (see p. 11). If we but connect to that spirit, then our souls will prod us onward until we too can declare, "Let there be light!"

3

THE VACATED SPACE

Following the creation of the first Tzimtzum, God continued to withdraw His presence and expand the size of the Vacated Space. Within that Vacated Space He proceeded to create, form and make the various worlds, of which there are five: *Adam Kadmon* (Primordial Man), *Atzilut* (Nearness or Emanation), *Beriyah* (Creation), *Yetzirah* (Formation) and *Asiyah* (Action). In our world, which is part of *Asiyah*, God created the galaxies, the solar system, planet Earth and man. God also created the Ten *Sefirot* (Luminaries, Illuminations or Energies), with which He directs the world (see p. 49).

The Vacated Space represents an area devoid of Godliness, since God contracted Himself from that space to "make room" for the Creation. However, the truth is that no place can exist without Godliness to sustain it. Therefore, God must be in that void. But if He is there, then it is not a Vacated Space! So God cannot be there. Yet He must be.... This is the paradox of the Vacated Space.

Rebbe Nachman teaches:

> God created the world out of His deep compassion. He wished to reveal His compassion, but without a world, to whom could He

34

show it? He therefore brought the entire Creation into existence, from the highest emanation down to the lowest point within the center of the physical world, all in order to demonstrate His compassion.

When God wished to create the worlds, however, there was no place in which to do so. This was because all that existed was His Infinite Essence, which precluded the existence of anything finite. He therefore constricted His Light. By virtue of this Tzimtzum, a Vacated Space was brought into existence. It was within this Vacated Space that everything was brought into being.

The Vacated Space was absolutely necessary for Creation. Without it, there would have been no place in which to create the universe. This Tzimtzum, which resulted in the Vacated Space, is at the moment incomprehensible to us. The only time we will be able to grasp its concept is in the Ultimate Future. This is because we can attribute to the Vacated Space only two mutually exclusive states—namely, existence and nonexistence.

The Vacated Space came into being as a result of the Tzimtzum, from which [to the extent that we can express it] God constricted (withdrew) His Essence. Therefore, God's Essence does not exist in this Space. If His Essence were there, this Space would not be vacated, and there would be nothing besides the Infinite Essence. If this were true, there would be no place whatsoever for the creation of the universe.

The actual truth, however, is that God's Essence must nevertheless be in this Space, for it is beyond any doubt that nothing can exist without His Life Force. Therefore, if God's Essence did not exist in the Vacated Space, nothing else could exist there either. It is impossible for any human being to understand the concept of the Vacated Space; only in the Ultimate Future will it be understood (*Likutey Moharan* I, 64).

The image of God withdrawing His Light (or Essence) should not be taken literally. God exists equally everywhere, at all times. "Withdrawing His Light" from the "Vacated Space" to "make room" for Creation in no way implies that He was, or is, no longer there. God was "there" equally, both before and after He created the

Vacated Space, and before and after He introduced the Kav (the Ray or Line that descends from the outer rim of the Vacated Space down to the exact center of the Vacated Space).[3]

The difference between "before" and "after" exists only from our vantage point—because the whole world was created only for the sake of mankind. The ARI says that the reason God created the Vacated Space was in order for man to have independent existence and free will. God certainly exists within all of Creation, for without Godliness nothing can exist. Yet if God's existence was clear and obvious in this world, man would not have free will. For this reason, God contracted His Light, as it were, to conceal Himself from man and make it *seem* as if there was a vacuum, a place devoid of Godliness.

With free will, a person can choose to serve God and perform good deeds, or to oppose God and transgress His directives. The existence of the Vacated Space within which God created worlds teaches us that our mission in life is also to be creative and build a better world—a better life for ourselves and for those with whom we come in contact. If we oppose God and refuse to accept our mission, we contradict the reason for Creation and essentially destroy that which others build, returning the world to a state of chaos and desolation, darkness and an abyss (cf. *Genesis* 1:2).

We might think there is a third option—to simply sit back and do neither good nor evil. However, the choice of "doing nothing" is not a valid option (cf. Rashi on *Numbers* 15:41). Since the Vacated Space is just that, a "hollow void," one who chooses not to do good and build, nor to do evil and destroy, will simply live out an empty existence. In the Ultimate Future, when others will claim their reward for their positive efforts, he may not receive punishment for wrongdoing, but he will experience an eternal void as "reward" for his lack of effort.

---

[3] Furthermore, God continues to exist within creation in an unchanging form, although creation itself is constantly in flux. This is another paradox of the Vacated Space.

Free will is a most incredible component of the entire Creation. Can anyone imagine a ruler who gives his subjects free rein to rise up in rebellion? Yet God created man with the intellect and the ability to turn against Him if he so desires! At the same time, the Vacated Space gives us the opportunity to emulate God by creating a life of good for ourselves, our neighbors and our environment. In simple terms, every person has his own "vacated space" within which he can exercise full control to build (or destroy) his own life.

Faith

"If you believe you can damage, believe you can repair!" (*Likutey Moharan* II, 112).

When it comes to building our lives, what works for one person doesn't necessarily work for another. Despite what was written in the Declaration of Independence, we are *not* created equal. We were all created by One God, yet each and every one of us is unique and has a different potential. Each of us has the ability to change his own life as well as the lives of those around him in a way no one else can.

So we try to develop *our* potential. We try our best, or second best, or third best, and put in effort to become someone, to advance and build a satisfactory life. How do we know we can succeed? What gives us the right to expect accomplishment? And what gives us the strength to keep trying? To answer these questions, we turn to another idea that is rooted in the Vacated Space, the concept of faith.

In general, faith denotes religion. We say that people subscribe to this faith or that faith, or even to no faith at all. Judaism, the basis of the Kabbalah, is founded upon four types of faith that are crucial to its observance:

1: Faith in God

2: Faith in the Torah

3: Faith in the Tzaddikim (righteous people)

4: Faith in Yourself

Obviously, faith in God is paramount. Without faith in God, we lack the crucial awareness that we are connected to the Infinite and therefore have an Infinite Resource to draw upon at all times and in all circumstances. This faith is extremely invigorating and encouraging, no matter what situation we find ourselves in or what is happening around us at any given moment, because through it we can access the One who created and controls all.

Faith in Torah is essential for attaining faith in God. Our heritage teaches us that the Torah is a product of God's Wisdom and is the blueprint for creating the world. God gave His Torah to the Jewish People at Sinai, so they could use it to harness and transform the material world into a vehicle for recognizing God in all circumstances. If we lack faith in the Torah, our connection to God and our ability to tap into the Infinite Resource is greatly weakened, since the only way we know about God is through His Torah.

Faith in the Tzaddikim helps us understand the Torah and its message and ultimately reach out to God. Our Sages teach that the Oral Torah was given together with the Written Torah (see p. 14); the Tzaddikim, masters of the Oral Torah, help us access the whole Torah. Their teachings open gateways to the deeper messages of the Torah and reveal to us the power that hovers beneath the surface of this world. This knowledge is essential for developing our potential, which also lies beneath the surface.

Without faith in yourself, however, the other types of faiths have little meaning. Why serve God? Why put in effort to study "old books" or the teachings of wise men of yore? What has this to do with me? Only if each of us believes, "I, as a person, was created by God, Who placed me on this planet with my unique strengths (and failings) and empowered me to accomplish whatever it is that I can while I am alive," then our lives take on real meaning. "Since He created me, He wants me! He loves me!" A person who believes he is important in God's eyes knows that he wasn't placed here randomly. He is alive for a reason; he has a purpose in life which he will learn about more and more as his life evolves. And along with his conviction that his life has purpose, he has faith in himself that he can accomplish and reach his goals.

Like the paradox of the Vacated Space, faith is also something that transcends reason: "I don't know if I can succeed, but I *believe* I can succeed." This idea is particularly important in light of the fact that Creation can only take place within a Vacated Space. This space represents a void, an unfamiliar territory in which we face life's challenges head-on. Being unsure of what to do next can be a frightening experience. But this is how we grow!

Generally speaking, people are creatures of habit. Facing a new challenge or confronting a new situation, a change in a relationship, a new job opportunity, etc., we almost always seek that which is familiar. It's natural to feel apprehensive about the unknown: "What does it mean to me?" "How will it affect my life?" So we seek the friendly or the usual. But we must not be afraid of the unknown. Apprehensive? Of course. But afraid? No! We must realize that it is only within uncharted territory—our personal "vacated space" and "hollow void"—that creation can take place and our potential can develop.

The following story illustrates this point:

> An automobile magnate once interviewed an engineer who sought employment with his company. The two went out to dinner and ordered steaks. While they were waiting to be served, they discussed the job arrangements. When the steaks arrived, the engineer proceeded to liberally salt his portion before he tasted it. The magnate told him that he would not be hired after all, saying, "If you will not try out something new without resorting to your lifetime habits, you are not creative enough for us!"

Life is full of challenges. Some we might relish; others we most certainly try to avoid. But we do not really have a choice about what we are about to face. Things have a way of being tossed into our lives at the most inopportune times and in the most unexpected ways. If we believe in ourselves, if we are positive about our ability to think clearly and reach responsible decisions using our available resources and knowledge, then we can face just about any situation and turn it into a new and beautiful creation.

Creating Our Own "Vacated Space"

We have seen that one's potential lies in developing the thoughts that enter one's mind. We have also seen that the "vacated space" is that open field in which a person can form his own world. In a marvelous parallel to the original Act of Creation, the heart, when influenced by the thoughts of the mind, has the capacity to create its own "vacated space" within which new creation can occur.

Rebbe Nachman explains that this comes about through our ability to choose what to think. If we choose good thoughts of serving God and performing good deeds, we will develop positive tendencies and desires and help build the world. If we choose to think evil and immoral thoughts, we fill the hollow of our hearts with spiritual and emotional pollution. Taking our potential in that direction will lead to the development of negative desires and the contamination of our world.

If we clearly saw the results of our choices, we would be hard-pressed not to choose good and serve God. If we clearly perceived God's Wisdom and greatness, we would be consumed with an irresistible desire to unite with His Infinite Light. Knowing that our very souls are rooted in God and that His breath connects us directly to Him, we would never want to be removed from His presence. Indeed, it is this unique relationship with God that gives us our potential to begin with.

In order to develop our potential, however, we must first experience a tzimtzum, a constriction of Godliness, and create a "vacated space" of our own in which to operate. Just as God's Light was everywhere, yet He carved out a Vacated Space to make "room" for Creation, we must "make room" for a "good creation" in our hearts, into which Godliness can enter and dwell. We do this by thinking good thoughts and eliciting higher and better levels of consciousness. Then we can merit an even greater revelation of Godliness.

In fact, when we turn our hearts into a "vacated space" to receive Godliness, we can form new creations simply by thinking good thoughts. Then we can rise to the level of performing miracles—in emulation of the original miracle of Creation (see *Likutey Moharan* I, 49:4,13).

4

THE SHATTERING OF THE VESSELS

As the next stage in Creation, God formed Ten Sefirot to act as channels or filters to convey His Light and Bounty. These Ten Sefirot were necessary tools in His plan, for without them, God's Infinite Light would have overwhelmed and obliterated worlds and creatures that were placed at lower levels of holiness and spirituality.

One more step was necessary, though, before the creation of the lower worlds could proceed apace. The prospect that these lower worlds would receive a continuous supply of Divine Light ran counter to another goal of Creation, which was that man should have free will. As the ARI explains (*Etz Chaim* 8:6), were God's Infinite Light always manifest, man would not have free will. If a person were always aware of God's presence, transgressing His Will would be impossible. God therefore concealed His Light, and in so doing allowed man to choose freely between doing good and doing evil.

Towards this end, God designed the original Ten Sefirot with a built-in flaw. A Sefirah consists of both light and a vessel (a lesser light that acts as a receptacle for the greater light). God designed the original Sefirah-vessels as separate entities that were incapable of giving support to one another. When He shone His Light into these vessels, the vessels could not bear the intensity of that influx, and shattered. Some of the shards were thrown far afield and formed *kelipot* (forces of evil), giving rise to an outside realm in which God's presence is almost totally hidden. The existence of these kelipot creates a balance of good and evil in Creation, enabling man to have free choice in his life.

After the Shattering of the Vessels, God "redesigned" the Sefirot so that the vessels would not be overwhelmed by the Light, but would be able to contain and filter the Light down to our world. At the same time, some of the shards of the shattered vessels descended to the lower realms in which the lower worlds—including planet Earth—were to be created. These shards, known as "sparks of holiness," were scattered throughout the creation. Later, when Adam ate from the forbidden Tree of Knowledge of Good and Evil, he caused further blemish to these sparks of holiness, casting them even farther away. One of man's spiritual missions is to gather up those sparks from wherever they may be and elevate them to their original level. We accomplish this mission by means of Torah study, prayer and the performance of good deeds.

Just as the Shattering of the Vessels took place on a macrocosmic level, it also takes place on a microcosmic level in every individual. Each new beginning creates its own tzimtzum. And each tzimtzum is followed immediately by a "drawing of the light" and a "shattering of the vessels." Moreover, each person possesses sparks of holiness that are unique to his psyche and that are affected by his environment, upbringing and education. With the "good" in Creation represented by accomplishing our goals and the "evil" in Creation represented by the challenges and frustrations we face along the way, let us apply the lessons of the Shattering of the Vessels to our daily lives.

How many times do we begin anew, making a fresh start with new zest and great confidence? Yet before very long, our resolve weakens and we find ourselves losing those great intentions? If we strengthen our resolve and take the first steps towards our goal, the realization that we can't achieve that goal immediately tends to break our resolve again. All this indicates that the "light" of potential is too "intense." We haven't prepared ourselves properly with the necessary "vessels"—i.e., the complete resolve to see our goal through to completion.

Moreover, the frustrations, challenges and obstacles that crop up on all sides put a damper on our plans, as if to say, "The shards and broken pieces of the shattered vessels—of my past mistakes and faulty judgments—keep getting in the way." Of course there will be obstacles to any worthy goal, and it is true that they stem from our mistakes, but we cannot let them deter us from achieving what is rightfully ours. Rather than view them as problems, we should view them as challenges that can rejuvenate our resolve to propel ourselves to greater heights. Whenever we see our good desires petering out, we must "redesign" our thought processes to tackle what lies ahead.

Additionally, the "sparks of holiness" teach us how to strengthen ourselves and succeed in our efforts. Since these sparks exist as a part of our psyches, we eventually come into contact with more and more of them at different stages of our lives. These sparks provide us with new insights and ideas for moving forward in life. Whenever we experience a "shattering" (i.e., confront an obstacle that throws us off course), we can rethink our approach, reevaluate our attempts, and either strengthen our resolve to continue in our original quest or conceive a fresh approach to the same problem.

Reb Noson notes that the story of Adam eating the forbidden fruit and causing more damage to the sparks of holiness carries an important personal message. During the course of our lives, we will do many good deeds; it's also more than likely that we'll "mess up" here and there. Whenever we do something wrong, we cause a microcosmic "shattering of the vessels" and a further spreading-out of the sparks of holiness.

This seems like a never-ending problem, with each mistake or intentional misdeed breaking our vessels into even more and tinier pieces. Yet it can also serve as a great source of comfort for those who truly desire to make something of their lives. From failure we learn that the goals we sought were too big or beyond reach. Each "shattering" serves to break those attempts into smaller goals— into attainable goals! Eventually, despite many upsets, those who continually seek to achieve will reach a low point that will then catapult them to great heights of success in their endeavors (*Likutey Halakhot, Birkhot HaReiach* 4:45).

In this way we can mirror the Act of Creation, rebuilding and restoring our "shattered vessels" in our attempt to realize our goals.

Part Three

THE ENERGIES OF
THE SEFIROT

1

THE TEN SEFIROT

Here we present a brief summary of the powers of the Sefirot as applies to our studies in this book. Many of the ideas which we will use to illustrate the energies of the Sefirot are explained in detail in *Innerspace* by Rabbi Aryeh Kaplan, and are being used with permission of Moznaim Publishers. For a deeper study of the Kabbalah and the human body, see *Anatomy of the Soul* by Chaim Kramer, Breslov Research Institute.

The ARI tells us that after God constricted His essence and created the Vacated Space, He drew a single, straight Kav (Ray or Line) down from His Infinite Surrounding Light into the Vacated Space. Through this Kav, the Supernal Light was drawn down and spread out in the universes that would be created. The Kav descended in stages, known as Sefirot.

Ten in number, the Sefirot contain the energies that infuse everything in Creation. The Sefirot also represent the powers and forces with which a human being can "make" his own life, developing his potential and actualizing his goals. Of the Sefirot, some are said to represent "mentalities" or "thought processes," while others represent "characteristics," "attributes" or "instruments" via which we can transform our thoughts into reality.

These are the names of the Ten Sefirot,[4] listed in descending order:

1: Keter (Crown)

2: Chokhmah (Wisdom)

3: Binah (Understanding)

   (Daat) (Knowledge)

4: Chesed (Lovingkindness)

5: Gevurah (Strength)

6: Tiferet (Beauty)

7: Netzach (Everlasting)

8: Hod (Splendor)

9: Yesod (Foundation)

10: Malkhut (Kingship)

In Kabbalistic thought, the Sefirot diffuse the Light of the Infinite as it filters down to this material world in a manner that can be beneficial to all. They also represent the basic powers necessary for us to function. This is seen in the Hebrew spelling of the word SePhiRah, which shares the same root as SaPeiR (to communicate). Etymologically, the word is similar to SaPiR (brilliant or luminary), and is related to SaPhaR (border).

From our vantage point in a finite world, the concept of infinity is truly beyond conception. The Kabbalists, recognizing finite man's inability to reflect upon something infinite, therefore speak of God as the Light of the Infinite. The Sefirot bridge the distance

---

[4] The discerning reader will note that eleven Sefirot are listed. The ARI explains that Daat is a quasi-Sefirah, since it represents the external manifestation of Keter. Wherever the functions of Keter are mentioned, the first three Sefirot are referred to as Keter, Chokhmah and Binah. When the Kabbalah speaks generally of the three higher Sefirot, then they are referred to as Chokhmah, Binah and Daat.

between the Infinite and the finite by channeling and modulating God's Infinite Light as it descends to our world. Since too much holiness at one time would overwhelm the material world, the Sefirot diffuse God's Light to ever-diminishing degrees, starting at the highest level of Keter and ending at the lowest Sefirah, Malkhut. Malkhut is the "acting agent" or interface between God and His Creation. From this level, God's Light is dispensed to this world in the form of spiritual awareness and material bounty.

The Sefirot are not a one-way street. As the interface between God and His Creation, Malkhut also represents the power to receive each person's offerings from this material world and send them upward to God. Thus the Sefirot act as interfaces of varying degrees between God and man. They diffuse the "brilliance" of God's Light into diminishing levels of intensity so that we can receive that Light in parameters (i.e., "borders") that we can relate to. They also act as the means of "communication" between God and man and between man and God.

In our context, the Sefirot represent the various powers and energies through which we can express our thoughts and desires and exercise our capabilities. They are the essential tools with which we can develop our potential and attain our goals. The upper Sefirot of Keter, Chokhmah, Binah and Daat, which are also known as the *Mochin* (Intellects), stand at the level at which the awesome power of our potential begins. Study of these Sefirot yields clues to the basis of our creativity, willpower and ability to act. The seven lower Sefirot of Chesed, Gevurah, Tiferet, Netzach, Hod, Yesod and Malkhut, also known as the *Midot* (Attributes or Characteristics), stand at the level at which our potential comes into actuality. Study of these Sefirot reveals techniques for channeling self-control, empathy and morality into achieving our goals.

To appreciate the practical application of the Sefirot in our day-to-day lives, let us explore their physical parallel in the human body, and their operation according to the principle of opposing energies.

Human Parallels

"And God created man in His image…in a Godly image did He create him, male and female He created them" (*Genesis* 1:27).

God has no form or image, nor can anything be used to depict Him in any manner whatsoever (*Rambam, Hilkhot Yesodei HaTorah*, Chapter 1). So what is meant by God creating man "in His image"? This expression refers to the Ten Sefirot which God used to create and establish everything in the universe. The Kabbalah teaches that each Sefirah has both a physical parallel in the human body and a conceptual parallel in the intellect, as follows:

Sefirah	Physical Representation	Conceptual Representation
Keter	cranium	will, purpose
Chokhmah	right brain/brain	mind, axioms
Binah	left brain/heart	logic
[Daat]	[brain stem/spine]	[connection]
Chesed	right arm/hand	benevolences, giving
Gevurah	left arm/hand	judgment, restraint
Tiferet	torso	truth, harmony
Netzach	right leg	victory, endurance
Hod	left leg	empathy, submission
Yesod	sexual organ	covenant, channel
Malkhut	mouth, mate	authority, receiving, reciprocity

Note that the upper Sefirot represent intellects and thought processes, while the lower Sefirot, from Chesed on down, represent characteristics. This is important to remember when we examine how the energies of the Sefirot correspond to the way man uses

THE TEN SEFIROT

those powers. It is also important to note that the anthropomorphic descriptions are only depictions of the Sefirot—neither they nor God have any image and it cannot be said that they have a head, arms, legs, etc. However, by schematizing the Sefirot in an anthropomorphic fashion, we can begin to visualize a system of greater and lesser energies and how each fits perfectly in its place.

The verse cited above refers to God's creation of "male and female." This manner of creation does not apply only to human beings. Our Sages teach that God created everything in this world as male and female, including members of the animal, vegetable and mineral kingdoms (*Bava Batra* 74b; see commentaries). It also applies to the Sefirot, which are designated as either "male" or "female" energies in a three-column system, with the center column representing a merging of these energies, as follows:

Left Column (Feminine Principle)	Center Column (Interaction-Harmony-Union)	Right Column (Masculine Principle)
	Keter	
Binah	[Daat]	Chokhmah
Gevurah	Tiferet	Chesed
Hod		Netzach
	Yesod	
	Malkhut	

This division of the Sefirot is not random. Both the assignment of male and female energies and the three-column system reveal the source of the Sefirot's powerful energy.

Firstly, the concept of male and female reflects the idea of interrelationships and "give and take." The Talmud (*Niddah* 31b) explains that the Hebrew word for male, *ZaKhaR*, indicates *Zeh KaR* (this is a gift), alluding to the role of a benefactor. The Hebrew word for female, *NeKeVaH*, connotes *NaKi VaH* (she has come empty-handed), indicating a recipient or beneficiary. In order for the world to survive, there will always be "benefactors" and "beneficiaries."

A union between husband and wife illustrates these roles in practice. It is the male who gives the seed and the female who receives it. However, these roles are not immutable. When the seed is received and developed into a child, then the female assumes the role of benefactor and the child is the beneficiary. The same can apply to a family. A husband might bring home income which the wife uses to buy food for the family. Here the husband is the benefactor and the wife is the recipient. But when the wife serves the meal, she becomes the benefactor while the husband is the beneficiary.[5]

Similarly, when a farmer sows a field, he is "giving" the earth seed and is considered to be the benefactor. But when the earth yields its fruits, it becomes the benefactor while the farmer is the beneficiary. Our bodies and souls connote the same relationship. The soul (benefactor) animates the body (beneficiary). But it is only because the body eats and draws nourishment that the soul remains with it. Thus the body becomes the benefactor while the soul is the recipient.

On the highest scale, God is The Benefactor, bestowing life, blessing and bounty, and mankind is the beneficiary. But when we perform good deeds and give God the *nachat* (joy and pleasure) of obeying His Will, then we become the benefactors and God becomes The Beneficiary.

Only when the concepts of benefactor and beneficiary interact can production evolve. This is a key idea in the process of bringing forth our potential. We must know when to take the next step

---

[5] Medically speaking, we find that all males have a certain amount of estrogen, the female hormone, while all women have some testosterone, the male hormone. This is because each human has an established role to act out—but that role is forever changing according to circumstances. Thus, "Male and female He created them."

forward, just like a benefactor who assesses and prepares to fulfill someone else's needs. We must also know when to take a step back, just like a beneficiary who might be overwhelmed or embarrassed. At times we must press forward to see our ideas materialize, and at times realize that pressing forward is a mistake and it is time to back off.

By themselves, male and female energies are insufficient to channel new creation. If they are unequally balanced, one will overpower the other and its stance will prevail. If they are evenly balanced, they will stand off head-to-head, propelling each one's ideas into the realm of argument and indecision. If a wife wants to hire a contractor to build a new kitchen but her husband wants to save money and do it himself, the force of each person's opinion is enough to ensure a long spat rather than a workable solution. To achieve a positive result, opposing energies must first face off and then coalesce in a harmonious manner.

The three-column system exemplifies this dynamic. Some Sefirot represent the right/male column, others represent the left/female column, and still others parallel the center/united column. In their normative state, the Sefirot are always divided into these three columns, which represent a state of equilibrium and allude to balance and stability in our lives. To effect change and growth, however, the Sefirot divide into two columns: "right and left," "male and female." These divided energies create powerful tension between the opposing sides. To properly develop these energies, we must strike a balance between them—a mutually beneficial formation of those opposing forces—to create a harmonious atmosphere. When both sides work together, potential can be actualized. The basic principle is found in Newton's Third Law of Physics: "For every action, there is an equal and opposite reaction."

The body and soul interact on the same principle of balance and counterbalance. By itself, each serves no purpose. A soul without a body has no place in this corporeal world, while a body without a soul is a lifeless form. Additionally, they are opposing forces. The soul strives continuously for spiritual attainments, shying away from material delights; the body always seeks physical pleasures while subjugating the soul's spiritual yearnings. Yet when these two opposing forces interact, they are most creative.

Reb Noson illustrates the interaction of body and soul using the analogy of an old-fashioned mechanical watch that must be wound each day. As the spring uncoils, its tension causes the gears of the watch to turn. Each gear, its teeth working against the teeth of a second gear, moves yet another gear, causing the watch to work with precision and keep accurate time. The same is true for all mechanical devices, which are built with gears that work against the direction of adjacent gears. Precisely because of the contraposition of the gears can these devices work effectively. The same is true of the body and soul—it is specifically their contraposition, when they are stimulated to work for a mutually beneficial goal, that makes them productive (*Likutey Halakhot, Yom Tov* 5:1).

Therefore God created each Sefirah/energy with its opposing Sefirah/energy so that in the vacuum between these opposing energies, man can develop his potential. We must learn to control these energies in order to cause them to act in a harmonious manner. Our "how to" manual is encapsulated in none other than the Torah.

The Sefirot and Torah

"This is the Torah, man…" (*Numbers* 19:14).

It is well known that the Torah contains 613 mitzvot (*Makkot* 23b). The root meaning of the verb *leTZaVot* (to command) is "to bind." When we perform a *miTZVah*, we bind ourselves and the world around us to God. The 613 mitzvot divide into 248 positive commandments and 365 prohibitions. These commandments encompass every aspect of our relationship with God, with our fellow human beings, and with all existence. Through the commandments, God provided every necessary tool with which we can connect to Him and bring all of creation to its Ultimate Goal.

The human form has 248 limbs—corresponding to the 248 positive commandments of the Torah—and 365 connecting tissues, veins or sinews—corresponding to the 365 prohibitions of the Torah (*Zohar* I, 170b). Thus, man's "Godly image," which parallels the Ten Sefirot, was fashioned in the pattern of the Torah. Not only his soul, but the very body that seemingly prevents him from rising above the physical limitations of this world, is a "Torah." Through this connection, man can utilize all that is contained in the world to recognize and serve God. With his soul, he can ascend beyond the material world and enter the realm of the spirit. With his body, he can channel the spiritual down into the material, creating the harmony that human life was meant to achieve.

The Torah is the link that allows us to develop our true potential. Reb Noson elaborates:

> In order to effect a remedy, a physician must have complete knowledge of the human anatomy. He must know all the parts of the body—the limbs, arteries, veins, etc. He must know how each and every organ is interconnected and interdependent with the others. He must be aware of how each organ can be affected by every other. Then, and only then, can a physician understand the nature of the illness and attempt healing. In the same vein, the Torah is a body of laws with each individual mitzvah representing an "organ" of that "body." To be able to fathom the true value of the Torah, a person must know its "anatomy"—its laws and ideals—how each mitzvah is interconnected with the others, as an individual, integral part of an entire Torah (*Likutey Halakhot, Rosh Chodesh* 5:6).

Reb Noson continues his discourse explaining the parallels between the Torah's "anatomy" and the human anatomy. This is a major theme found in the Kabbalah, which describes the connection between certain parts of the body and certain mitzvot. Reb Noson writes elsewhere that one who understands the writings of the Zohar and the ARI will realize that all the mysteries of the Kabbalah speak about the deep connection between the Torah and mitzvot, the Ten Sefirot and the human who can harness his energies and reveal this awesome power, the "Godly image" (see *Likutey Halakhot, Minchah* 7:22).

With these basics in mind, let us now turn to an in-depth study of the nature and characteristics of each Sefirah. We will supplement each study with important teachings of Rebbe Nachman on how to best apply these energies to our daily lives.

2

KETER
The Light of Will

Keter is the first and highest of the Sefirot. *Keter* means crown, indicating that it "sits above" the other Sefirot and represents absolute authority, that of the king and master. Just as in human hierarchies, where there are many levels between a monarch and his subjects, Keter represents the highest level between God and us. In order for its authority to be realized, however, it must be filtered into a vessel that can reveal it. Thus, the energy of Keter must be filtered down through several levels until it reaches the lowest level, that of Malkhut. In Malkhut, its might and power can be displayed.

Keter is the interface between God and His Creation. It is from that highest of levels that the spiritual energies devolve into the lower realms until they materialize or become actualized in the physical world to which we are accustomed.

Throughout the Kabbalah, God is referred to as the Ein Sof (The Infinite), and sometimes as Ayin (Nothingness—for nothing can truly describe God). By extension, Keter, which acts as the interface with God, is also called Ayin. This reference is not random, since

THE ENERGIES OF THE SEFIROT

the Sefirah of Keter represents the loftiest levels of humility and self-negation. When a person acts humbly, he invokes the energy and attribute of Keter.

Keter is said to parallel the concept of will and/or purpose. Keter is a code word for God's Will, the ultimate reason and cause for which He brought the world into existence, as well as the final purpose and goal (i.e., His Master Plan) towards which Creation is headed. In Keter, God has created a force that drives everything in creation. He set up rules that govern the world, subjecting everything in creation to His specific dictates (such as the forces of nature). Yet when He wills it, He can force nature itself to divulge that God is in charge. An example would be the Splitting of the Sea (see *Exodus* 14)—a physical impossibility, yet something that did take place and that was witnessed by many millions of people.

Keter is associated with our free choice to will the goals we seek into our lives. On the level of Keter, we are compelled neither by internal predisposition nor by external circumstances; our decisions are completely independent of all other considerations. This is because our willpower emanates from our essence, that inner or spiritual part of us that resembles God. When we connect to this deep level of inner volition, we can "move mountains" and find the ability to do almost anything! This is the idea behind our near-limitless potential.

The concept of free choice presents us with a paradox, however. God has His Master Plan, yet man can choose to act according to the dictates of his own heart. In fact, God's knowledge of the future in no way deprives us of the chance to exercise our right to choose freely. This paradox is encapsulated in the concept of Keter, a level beyond anything we can understand.

At every turn, we can choose a path that either coincides with God's Master Plan or goes against it. It matters not, for God too has "Free Will." Depending on *His* choice, God will either allow our choice to stand, or set up adverse conditions. Then a test of "wills" comes to the fore.[6]

In the end, God's Will *will* win out. The more determined we are to challenge God's Will, the greater our chances of obscuring the Light of Keter. If we take that course, we will face much adversity without the side benefits of personal growth. Alternately, the more we try to act in accordance with God's Will, the greater will be our contribution towards bringing about that Master Plan, and the more obvious will be the role that Divine Providence plays in our lives. We will then be more aware of the reason for adversity in life and be better equipped to receive the blessings hidden within that adversity (the tzimtzum). Simply put, we will be more in tune with the Source of our potential and thus better able to develop it.

Let us turn to the teachings of Rebbe Nachman to understand the four key attributes that Keter represents, and how we can access them on a daily basis.

Will

To develop our potential, we must have a desire and a purpose to develop it. Keter is that energy of will or purpose.

To introduce Rebbe Nachman's understanding of will and desire, Reb Noson recorded a conversation that he once had with him:

"You do speak with people," the Rebbe said. "You probably ask them *what*."

He emphasized the word *what*, stressing it in a loud voice from the depths of his heart: "*What?*"

"It is fitting to ask people this question if they do not think of their purpose in life. *What?*

---

[6] Reb Noson explains that free will is so powerful that we can sometimes "force" God to give in to our choice! We must be very sure about what we want, however, and that the consequences will be good for us, before we invest all our energy in "convincing" God that we need something (see *Likutey Halakhot, Birkhot HaShachar* 5:76-78).

"You have many vain and foolish complaints and excuses. Your life is filled with confusion and frustration. *What?*

"*What* will become of you? *What* will you do in the end? *What* will you answer the One Who sent you? *What* do you think? *What* are you on earth if not a stranger? *What* is your life, if not vanity and emptiness, 'a passing shadow, a scattered cloud' (*Rosh HaShanah Liturgy*)?

"You know this well. What do you say?

"Place these words well on your heart. Bring them into the depths of your being. Do not ignore them. Turn them over and over and you will save your soul" (*Rabbi Nachman's Wisdom* #286).

Rebbe Nachman was always concerned about not wasting time, of never wasting a minute of life. If we examine the goals that most of us live by, however, we may be surprised to find that our energies are being misspent. Most of us spend our whole lives working in order to earn money for material comforts, then old age sets in, then sickness prevails and death follows. Of what use to us are such material goals?

Rebbe Nachman observes:

This world exists only to bring about God's purpose. Do not be concerned with wealth. Even with it our lives can be in vain. The world deceives us completely. It makes us think that we are constantly gaining, but in the end we have nothing. People spend years earning money, but are left with empty hands. Even one who attains wealth has it taken away from him. Man and money cannot endure together. Either money is taken from the man, or the man is taken from his money. The two do not remain together. Where are all the riches accumulated since the beginning of time? People have amassed money since the beginning—where is it all? It is absolutely nothing (*Rabbi Nachman's Wisdom* #51).

The Rebbe is quite clear about where we should concentrate our energies. While everything in Creation has a purpose, he explains, the Ultimate Goal of the entire creation and the reason for everything that exists is the delight of the World to Come. However, the only minds that are capable of comprehending and grasping this purpose are those of the Tzaddikim. Each person, in accordance with the root that he has in the soul of the Tzaddik, can learn more about the purpose of Creation from the latter to the degree that he breaks his anger with compassion (*Likutey Moharan* I, 18:2).

The idea of "breaking anger with compassion" is a cornerstone of patience. Instead of "losing it" by becoming frustrated and angry, we must learn to temper our impatience, creating a tranquil atmosphere in which to concentrate on our goal.

We face so many temptations. The desire for wealth can divert our will. Food, moral issues and countless other provocations confront us daily. Only when we harness the energy of Keter (will and desire) can we begin to focus on what is right and what is wrong.

Rebbe Nachman explains that our souls are actually formed through the yearning and desire that we feel for God and our good intentions to serve Him. No matter what our level, each of us has a desire to reach a higher level. It is through this yearning that our holy souls are formed (*Likutey Moharan* I, 31:6-7). Moreover:

> All the barriers that a person encounters are only for the sake of desire—that is, in order that he should have a greater desire for the holy thing that he wishes to do. It is human nature that the more a person is restrained from doing something, the more he desires to do it. Therefore, when you need to do something that is integral to your life as a Jew, and particularly when you need to do that thing upon which your entire Judaism may depend—namely, to travel to the true Tzaddik—at that time you are granted desire from Above. This desire is granted through the barrier that confronts you, since as a result of that barrier, your desire increases. Therefore, know that there is no barrier in the world that you cannot break if you really want to, and you will undoubtedly merit to complete the task (*Likutey Moharan* I, 66:4).

The genesis and development of potential is actually a conditioned response. To arouse the desire in our hearts, God stimulates positive thoughts in our minds to direct our will towards "creation." But will is a forceful energy that can arouse negative characteristics which thwart the realization of potential. Our task is to pit the former against the latter, constantly spurring our desire to overcome barriers and strengthen our desire more. As the Talmud teaches (*Makkot* 10b), "On the road a person wishes to travel, he will be led."

Life consists of material needs that are temporary, and spiritual necessities that are everlasting. As such, Rebbe Nachman focuses on the need to do something integral to being a Jew, to experience life in the here and now, and yet reap long-lasting benefits. Weighing our use of will for long-lasting gain as opposed to temporal pleasure will guarantee the receipt of positive messages from Above and set us on the right road to developing our potential.

Rebbe Nachman adds: "You must totally nullify your own will before God's Will and have no other wish except for what God wishes. Whether you have money and children or otherwise, God forbid, you must still only desire what God desires. When you are satisfied with only that which God desires, then you make God King over yourself" (*Likutey Moharan* I, 177).

Similarly, the Zohar teaches: "The structure of a human being parallels the structure of Creation. This is why Man is known as a microcosm of the world. When one accepts God's reign [the purpose of Creation] upon each and every organ of his body, it is as if he has established God's Sovereignty over the whole world" (*Tikkuney Zohar* #70, p. 130b). The idea is to focus on the Real Power behind our deeds and synchronize our desires so that we are capable of receiving God's messages and defining them correctly. And we must learn to define that power correctly because, as Rebbe Nachman teaches, "Everything you see in the world—everything that exists—is all a test to give man freedom of choice" (*Rabbi Nachman's Wisdom* #300).

Another tool that can help us develop our will is the observance of the Three Festivals: Pesach, Shavuot and Sukkot. The miraculous events that occurred on each of these festivals revealed the primacy of God's Will over the laws of nature, as God manipulated nature to perform awesome wonders for His people. Pesach commemorates the exodus of millions of Jews from Egypt—a near impossibility, considering the size and might of the Egyptian army—and the miraculous Splitting of the Sea, which took the Jews across on dry land while their enemies drowned. Shavuot heralds the Giving of the Torah, when God revealed Himself and spoke to the entire nation. Sukkot celebrates the miraculous Clouds of Glory that surrounded and protected the Jews during their forty years of wandering in the desert (*Likutey Moharan* II, 4:6).

Just as God transcends the laws of nature, we, in our own way, have the power to overcome seemingly "natural" barriers to achieve our goals. But we can only do so if we are in harmony with God's Will. We can develop that connection by observing the Three Festivals.

Humility

The Kabbalah speaks about Keter as being ineffable. It is so lofty an energy that it defies description. The Sages equate the energy of Keter with humility and self-negation before God. The more we attempt to nullify ourselves before God, the more we can invoke the energy of Keter.

To illustrate this concept, we quote our Sages (*Bava Batra* 25b): "Whoever desires wealth should face north [while praying], while whoever seeks wisdom should face south." In the Holy Temple, the *Shulchan* (Table, which symbolizes wealth) was positioned north of the entrance to the Holy of Holies, while the *Menorah* (Candelabrum, which represents wisdom) was positioned south of the entrance.

Rebbe Nachman observes that a person who is in one place (i.e. north/wealth) cannot be in another (i.e., south/wisdom) at the same time. However, if one attains humility, he negates himself. He is "not in any place" since he considers himself as naught. That person can have all the advantages of the material world, since he does not have spatial requirements or limitations (*Likutey Moharan* I, 162).

Through humility, one can even "shed his physicality and be included in the Infinite," the Rebbe adds. "He will know that everything that happens to him is for his good, which is a 'taste' of the World to Come" (*Likutey Moharan* I, 4:1).

Self-nullification opens a person to receiving as much of God's Infinite Light as He will bestow upon him. As such, humility acts as a "relay station," allowing us to receive God's energies to increase our potential, then enabling us to translate this increased potential into greater, more beneficial and profitable deeds.

How can we achieve this level of humility? Rebbe Nachman teaches us how:

> The main thing is to nullify every one of your personality traits. You must strive to do so until you have totally obliterated your ego, rendering it into absolute nothingness before God. Begin with one trait and annihilate it completely. Then work on your other traits, one at a time, until they are totally nonexistent. As you annihilate your own personality, God's glory will begin to shine through and be revealed.
>
> It is written (*Ezekiel* 43:2), "And the earth was alight with His glory." God's glory is like light. The larger an object, the greater its shadow. A thin rod casts a very small shadow, while a more substantial object casts a larger shadow. A great building will cast an even larger shadow. As more light is obstructed, a greater shadow is cast. The same is true of God's glory. The material obstructs the spiritual and casts a shadow. The denser an object, the deeper a shadow it will cast. When you are bound to an emotion or desire, it obstructs God's glory and casts a shadow. God's Light is then hidden from you. But as you nullify these emotions and desires, you also remove this shadow. And as the shadow departs, the light of God's glory is revealed.
>
> When a man is worthy of annihilating the shadow completely and making it into absolute nothingness, then God's glory is revealed to all the earth. There is no obstructing shadow, and the light can shine through in all its glory. It is written (*Isaiah* 6:3), "*MeLoA ha'aretz Kevodo*—The whole earth is filled with His glory." This can also be read, "*MiLoA*—From *nothing* is all the earth His glory." When there is nothing—nothing casting a shadow or obstructing His Light— then His glory is revealed everywhere (*Rabbi Nachman's Wisdom* #136).

On the one hand, Rebbe Nachman speaks of attaining humility to experience God in His Infinite greatness and to channel His limitless energy into our lives. On the other hand, the Rebbe clearly delineates the damaging effects of humility's opposite—i.e., haughtiness or pride—which limits and even deflects the energy of Keter. Pride forces God out of the picture, restricting our ability to benefit from His energy to achieve our goals.

Pride gives rise to doubts that can engulf a person and confuse his faith, effectively causing God to depart from that person's presence. Thus the Talmud teaches (Sotah 4b) that God says to the proud man, "You and I cannot abide together." Rebbe Nachman adds that pride is tantamount to idol worship, for it precipitates the loss of the faculties of speech that could have enabled a person to speak in a way that radiates God's Light. Indeed, the person may not be able to open his mouth at all, or that which emerges from his mouth has no tangible value (Likutey Moharan I, 11:3).

The antidote to pride is simple: "Open your eyes. If you compare your own lowly state to God's lofty greatness, you will never be proud or skeptical" (Rabbi Nachman's Wisdom #261).

When we evaluate where we stand on the scale of humility versus pride, we may feel we come up short. Should we begin to view ourselves as unworthy, however, we might never try to develop our enormous potential. To counter that tendency, the Rebbe teaches that the greatest revelation of God's glory comes through those who are furthest from Him, when they make the attempt to return and draw closer. No one should claim, "How can I come close to God, seeing that I am so removed from Him because of my wrongdoings?" because that is not true. God's glory is magnified precisely when that person begins to draw close again. For this reason, everyone is obligated to help others come closer to God (Likutey Moharan I, 14:2).

Reb Noson illustrates the value of humility in a most unusual manner. Trees and crops grow from seeds that are planted in the ground. Only after the seed has been covered with earth and left to decay does it takes root, sprout and produce great trees and life-sustaining crops. So it is with a human being. When he learns to negate himself and becomes as humble as the earth which everyone trods upon, he can begin to develop and grow and become a much greater person (Likutey Halakhot, Kila'ey HaKerem 2:1).

Patience

The origins of Creation—any creation—lie in the mystery of the tzimtzum, the necessary constriction before developing one's thought (see p. 29). This concept is embodied in the Hebrew word *KeTeR*, which also connotes *KaTaR*, an expression of waiting (see *Job* 36:2). Just as constriction implies holding back or focusing, we can best develop our thoughts and potential through the attribute of patience.

Rebbe Nachman explains the Sefirah of Keter as "the power of the human intellect to compose and organize the mind so that it does not hazard to go beyond its boundaries" (*Likutey Moharan* I, 24:9). We must organize our thoughts and intentions and not rush into things. But we shouldn't hesitate too long and miss opportunities for growth. Patience is necessary both to check the impulse to act immediately and to compose our thoughts before taking the next step forward.

God shows tremendous patience with the human race.[7] He always gives it time to develop its potential for the good, despite the presence of those who appear from time to time and make a mess of His world. When we exercise patience, we invoke Keter, the attribute of waiting, despite the adversity we face or the overwhelming urge to get beyond that challenge.

Rebbe Nachman offers several useful pieces of advice for those who wish to develop patience. He teaches: "Be long-suffering in all aspects of your character. Never become angry or irritated over anything. No matter what you have to go through, bear everything patiently without being blown off course. Let nothing make you lose your temper. Endure everything with patience, and simply do your own part to serve God with enthusiasm and joy" (*Likutey Moharan* I, 155).

Rebbe Nachman suffered from tuberculosis during the last three years of his life. In his final days, he had to be very careful about anything that would affect his lungs. Once, his attendant carelessly

---

[7] See *Gittin* 88b, where it states, "Speedily, in God's terms, is 850 years!"

allowed the fire he was kindling in the Rebbe's room to emit smoke. A short time later, Reb Noson, the Rebbe's closest disciple, entered the room. Seeing the smoke, he immediately extinguished the flame. Then he asked the Rebbe why he hadn't called someone to properly stoke the fire. Rebbe Nachman replied, "If I would have called out and no one had heard me, I might have become annoyed and angry. Better to suffer a little than to become angry."

One must strike a balance, however, between exercising patience and moving forward when the opportunity arises. Rebbe Nachman advises:

> When something can be done today, never leave it for tomorrow. The world does not stop even for a second. Anything you can do to serve God should be done immediately and determinedly, without delay. Who knows what obstacles—outer and inner—you will face if you leave it until later? Man's world consists only of the present.

> However, there are times when you see that in spite of all your efforts and determination, you cannot seem to succeed in what you want. Sometimes you must simply wait. Don't be discouraged because you are not achieving what you want. Don't let this push you off course. You must wait a little until the time comes. The only important thing is to look towards God at all times with longing and yearning, even when things are not going as well as you might like with your prayers and devotions. Never despair, no matter what. As soon as God gives you the opportunity to do something holy, do it immediately (*Tzaddik* #431).

As a caveat to this teaching, the Rebbe adds:

> Never insist that everything goes exactly the way you want— not even when what you want is genuinely holy. When you can do something immediately, you should certainly act swiftly. Something holy should never be delayed for a moment. On the contrary, you should make every effort to do it as quickly as possible. But if, in spite of everything, you still cannot do it at once, do not become anxious and agitated. Relax and wait quietly for God to help, and raise your eyes on high in the hope of succeeding in the end. God will almost always help you later on, to accomplish what you want (ibid., #433).

DON'T GIVE UP!

To illustrate the importance of patience, Rebbe Nachman once told a parable about a pair of hoboes, one Jewish, the other German, who were good friends and traveled the countryside together.

As the festival of Pesach approached, the Jew told his friend that a very good meal was in store for them. He encouraged the German to pretend he was a Jew (since the German tongue is similar to Yiddish), so that the Jewish townsfolk would have pity on him and invite him in for the Seder. The Jew also taught the German how to act at the Seder and explained the customs of that ritual meal: the recital of Kiddush over wine, then the washing of the hands, then the eating of a small piece of vegetable, then the recital of the Haggadah, then the second cup of wine, the second washing of the hands and the eating of matzah. Afterwards, a sumptuous meal would be served. However, he forgot to tell his friend about the *marror* (the bitter herbs).

The German was indeed invited to a house and, being very hungry, eagerly anticipated the fine foods his Jewish friend had described to him. After Kiddush, his host gave him a piece of celery dipped in salt water. While the family recited the Haggadah, the German sat there longing for the meal. Finally, when the matzah was served, he was very happy.

Then his host gave him a piece of horseradish, which was extremely bitter-tasting. Thinking that this was the entire meal, the German jumped up and ran from the house, bitter and hungry. "Cursed Jews!" he cried. "After all that ceremony, that's all they serve to eat?!" He made his way to the synagogue and fell asleep there.

After a while the Jew arrived, happy and full from a good meal. "How was your Seder?" he asked. The other told him what had happened. "You foolish German!" replied the Jew. "Had you waited just a little longer, you would have had a fine meal, as I had" (*Rabbi Nachman's Stories, Parable #23*).

This is what happens to us, Rebbe Nachman says, when we want to come close to God. After all the effort we make to get started, we experience a little bitterness and lose our resolve. In fact, this bitterness is sent to purify the body so that it will be able to receive even more holiness. But a person might think that this bitterness is all there is to serving God, and runs away from it. Instead, he should exercise patience and wait a short while, allowing himself to be purified. Then he will be the happy recipient of every joy and delight in the world as he comes close to God.

Repentance

Obviously, when we draw strength from Keter, we take the first step towards moving forward in life. What happens, though, if we have misdirected our will or obscured the energy of Keter—say, by acting selfishly? Once botched, is that energy lost, or will it always be misguided?

The answer is an emphatic "No!" Prior to creating the world, God formed the character trait of regret, or as is more commonly known, repentance. It is possible to turn things around. Not only that, but there are times when we can emerge from those mistakes with an even more enhanced power of Keter.

As the first Sefirah, Keter connotes exactly that: "first," a new beginning. We can harness the energy of renewal and always make a fresh start. Recall Rebbe Nachman's teaching that God created the world in order to bestow His compassion on others (see p. 34). As God created the world, He can carry it, He can endure human defiance, and He can tolerate wrongdoing. His endless compassion extends to all, even to those who have sinned terribly. As the first emanation, Keter reflects that compassion and imparts that energy of regret, enabling us to rectify our mistakes and keep moving forward with our lives.

Rebbe Nachman emphasizes the lofty level of repentance this way:

You may fall to the lowest depths, Heaven forbid. But no matter how far you have fallen, it is still forbidden to give up hope. Repentance is higher even than the Torah, and therefore there is absolutely no place for despair. If you are worthy, even your worst sins can be turned into something good. We are taught that sins can be transformed into virtue. This idea may contain deep secrets, but the main lesson is that one's failings and shortcomings can easily be returned to God. Nothing is beyond His power. The most important thing is never to give up, but to continue to cry out and pray to God (Rabbi Nachman's Wisdom #3).

The idea of repentance poses many questions, not the least of which is how saying "I'm sorry" can change something that's already done. But the energy of Keter teaches us that God can subjugate anything in creation to His Will whenever He desires. When He reveals Himself, nature is forced to admit that God is really in charge. Thus, if a person errs in a specific time or place and then repents, God can alter that fact and bring forth from any wrongdoing a state of rectification. Though our human minds cannot understand how wrong can be turned into right, repentance is a powerful tool that God has implanted in Creation. Its source lies in the energy of Keter.

What applies to a single misstep also applies to those who have "messed up" their entire lives. By invoking the energy of Keter, which reflects the highest levels of compassion, we can begin again. We can find refuge from the past and be able to build a whole new future. Rebbe Nachman teaches: "Repentance helps for every conceivable sin—even the most serious of sins" (Rabbi Nachman's Wisdom #71).

Through humility, one merits repentance. For the essence of repentance is when a person hears himself being humiliated and he holds his peace and remains silent. He just accepts what he hears and understands that it is fitting that he suffer the insults" (Likutey Moharan I, 6:2).

The natural response to being hurt by others, or to feeling remorse from one's deeds, is to ignore or fight the pain. Instead, the

Rebbe recommends, let the energy of Keter do the work for you! When you feel hurt or remorse, react *positively* to those emotions. How? By remaining silent! In this way, the energy of Keter will begin to flow freely. A mistake means, "I must start again and it probably won't be easy." Keter means, "I need to invoke compassion! I need to somehow reconnect to my Source and start again!" Instead of answering—or even worse, retorting—begin your journey of self-renewal.

It's not easy to recognize when and where we can invoke the energy of Keter. From where do we start? The answer is: From wherever we are—even if we are at opposite poles from God.

> Even if a person is immersed in impurity and at an extremely low level, to the point that he imagines it is no longer possible for him to come close to God, since he has grown so very far from Him—even if he has fallen to actual atheism—nevertheless, he should know that even in this place he can still find Godliness, because "You give life to them all" (*Nehemiah* 9:6). Even from there he can still cleave to God and return to Him in perfect repentance. For God is not far away at all—it is just that in that place there are a great many "garments" concealing Him (*Likutey Moharan* I, 33:2).

> The more you feel that you are far from God's glory, the more you should ask and seek, "Where is the place of His glory?" Then, through the very fact that you feel this pain, that you search and yearn for God's glory and cry out, "Where is the place of His glory?" you will experience a very great ascent and rise to an extremely high level of holiness. This is the essence of repentance—namely, that you should constantly seek and search, "Where is the place of His glory?" and through this any descent is transformed into a very great ascent (*Likutey Moharan* II, 12).[8]

Keter is the beginning of the thought process. As will be explained below (see p. 80), thoughts are filtered through a person's heart, where they are exposed to one's emotions. As the person vacillates between thought and emotion, he learns to take control

---

[8] This important lesson is developed at length in a separate publication, *"Ayeh?"* published by Breslov Research Institute.

of his heart and focus on the right thing to do. Therefore Rebbe Nachman teaches:

> Repentance depends primarily on the heart, as implied in the phrase (*Isaiah* 6:10), "His heart will understand and he will repent." More specifically, it depends on the thoughts in your heart and that you strive to flee from bad thoughts and think good thoughts at all times. Truly take to heart what your final end will be, and think about methods and tactics by which to return to God.... When you repent and rectify the spiritual damage you may have done, you can also make up for the spiritual work you lost. Therefore, run swiftly and work zealously in your service of God in order to compensate for what you could have accomplished in the past (*Likutey Moharan* I, 49:5-6, end).

Repentance can also be accessed through one's mind. Rebbe Nachman explains that the Hebrew word for repentance, *teshuvah*, literally means return. Repentance means "to return a thing to the place from which it was taken—to restore it and return it to its root. Now, wisdom is the root of everything. This is why you must guard your mind and your wisdom against alien ideologies and extraneous thoughts, not to speak of evil temptations. The reason for all the sins and transgressions that people commit, and all their shortcomings, is that their thoughts are impure. They are not careful to guard their thoughts or avoid overstepping the bounds of holiness. When a person protects his thoughts and his wisdom, he can remedy everything and return to God" (*Likutey Moharan* I, 35:1).

By implication, Rebbe Nachman is saying that any attempt on our part to return to God will invoke the energy of Keter. And the energy of Keter enables a person to begin anew at all times! There should be no room for despair in any of our endeavors. The Rebbe encourages:

> This is an important rule in devotion: Never let yourself fall completely.

> There are many ways you can fall. At times your prayer and devotion may seem utterly without meaning. Strengthen yourself and begin anew. Act as if you were just beginning to serve God. No

matter how many times you fall, rise up and start again. Do this again and again, for otherwise you will never come close to God.

Draw yourself towards God with all your might. Remain strong, no matter how low you fall. Whether you go up or down, always yearn to come close to God. You may be brought low, but cry out to God and do everything you can to serve Him in joy. For without this inner strength, you will never be able to truly approach God (*Rabbi Nachman's Wisdom* #48).

Rebbe Nachman adjured his students to never despair or give up hope that they *could* better themselves and repair the past. He said: "When you look at me, you doubtless take me to be a perfect Tzaddik. Nevertheless, even if I were to commit the gravest possible sin, it would still not throw me at all. After sinning I would still be righteous, just as I was before. I would repent!" (*Tzaddik* #453).

Reb Noson reports:

There was one extraordinary occasion when the Rebbe spoke in awesome terms about the greatness of the Creator. He spoke in a way that is impossible to describe in writing. Immediately afterwards he began to give encouragement, saying that even if a person experiences a tremendous fall, each one in his own way, he should still strengthen himself and never despair, because God's greatness is exalted even beyond the Torah and there is a place where everything can be corrected. For repentance is beyond the Torah.

"But how can we achieve this?" I asked.

"It is possible to come to it," he replied, "as long as you never despair or give up crying out, praying and pleading. The only thing is to cry out, to pray, to plead...never, ever tire of it. Eventually you will rise up from where you have fallen. The essence of repentance is to cry out to God" (*Tzaddik* #565).

With a directed will, humility, patience and understanding of the power of repentance, we can direct the light and energy of Keter into our lives.

3

✤

THE MOCHIN
Overview

At different times we all experience "primal will," the idea of the Keter, which sets the stage for new creation in our lives. By itself, however, that initial urge or desire to create has no intrinsic value. Just as a child must first be conceived and then pass through the stages of embryo and fetus until it is completely formed and ready to be born into this world, every idea, concept and invention must pass through its own "embryonic stages" in order to be developed and revealed.

The tools which God used to chart, shape and refine the idea of Creation are the next three Sefirot: Chokhmah, Binah and Daat, known as the Mochin (Intellects). These three Sefirot also comprise the channels through which our own "first thought" is molded and refined into a workable plan. In the schematic representation of the Sefirot, Chokhmah, Binah and Daat are arrayed at the top just under Keter, filtering God's Light down to the seven lower Sefirot. Similarly, the human brain, or intellect, rests at the top of the body, from where it directs the activities of each of the lower organs and extremities.

While we normally think of the human intellect as one entity, it actually consists of several complementary functions. The Kabbalah isolates and defines three different aspects of intellect, corresponding to Chokhmah, Binah and Daat. Using these three functions, we too can analyze and transform our will into a concrete, doable plan.

4

CHOKHMAH, BINAH, DAAT
The Light of Perception

Chokhmah, Binah and Daat translate as Wisdom, Understanding and Knowledge, respectively. These three Sefirot are called the Mochin (Intellects) because they are the first revelation of the energy that descends from Keter. In our quest to develop our own potential, we must first direct and apply our intellects to the task.

Chokhmah, Binah and Daat correspond to the right and left brains and the brain stem, respectively. Chokhmah is undifferentiated wisdom, the facts without explanation (paralleling the right, "nonverbal" hemisphere). Binah is the understanding and analysis of those facts (paralleling the left, "verbal" hemisphere). Daat is the confluence of Chokhmah and Binah, the ability to apply that wisdom to the task at hand (paralleling the brain stem, which transfers the impulses of the brain to the rest of the body).

Chokhmah is called "beginning," as in (*Psalms* 111:10), "*Reishit chokhmah*—The beginning is wisdom." Chokhmah corresponds to the fundamental truths of reality that lie behind all our thought processes. These truths are both built into our minds at birth and integrated through our life experiences. For example, the axiom, "The shortest distance between two points is a straight line" implies that space exists, a point exists, straight lines exist, distance exists, and so on. Chokhmah corresponds to the latter truths, which depict the essence of things.

Binah is the logical system that connects these concepts and allows them to interact and emerge as a coherent system of laws. The Talmud (*Sanhedrin* 93b) defines Binah as "the ability to understand or distinguish one thing from another." *BiNah* is related to the Hebrew word *BeiN* (between), implying the ability to grasp underlying relationships. It is also related to the word *BoNeh* (build), as our intellect enables us to construct new concepts and systems.

On the level of Chokhmah, all that exists is undifferentiated potential or essence. Through Binah, the mind begins to differentiate, analyze and dissect into component parts. We may draw an analogy to water (Chokhmah) flowing through a system of pipes (Binah). Water itself is an "undifferentiated" fluid, having no essential macroscopic structure. Structure is imposed on it when it flows through the system of pipes.

In another sense, Chokhmah alludes to the past, while Binah refers to the future. This is seen in the Hebrew words for male and female. *ZaKHar* (male) has the same consonants as *ZoKHeR* (to remember). *NeKeVah* (female) has the same consonants as *NiKeV* (pierce or penetrate). The male "remembers" the past, while the female accesses the future. Both Chokhmah and the past can be explained in terms of the information we already possess. But the future exists only in our imaginative projections, which are a product of Binah. We must employ our Binah in order to "see" them.

While we might remember the past and anticipate the future, it is only the present that we know. The present moment, which lies at the confluence of the past (Chokhmah) and the future (Binah), corresponds to Daat. Daat is the focus of our perception.

In contrast to Chokhmah and Binah, which are completely internal processes (they are called "the hidden things"), Daat is an external manifestation, the ability to communicate one's thoughts effectively. Daat represents the power to interact with and develop an intelligent relationship with the outside world (see *Likutey Moharan* I, 25:1).

This explains why Daat manifests as the external cloak of Keter. In Keter, we have that primal will or instinct to act. But what are we supposed to act on? We call upon our resident wisdom, Chokhmah, to perceive the potential in that will. Then we analyze it with our Binah and begin to understand the energy it contains. Daat allows us to apply that will to a sensible and productive conclusion.

At the level of Chokhmah we find the most basic truths of existence standing in a kind of pristine unity. Binah is the system of logic by which the truths of Chokhmah are delineated and defined. Daat would then be called "applied logic," the manifestation of the inner mind.

Mind and Heart

Interestingly, we find throughout the Kabbalah that Chokhmah and Binah are also compared to the mind and the heart, respectively. In this construct, Chokhmah refers to intellectual wisdom and Binah to intuitive understanding.

Though there is much to be said for intuitive understanding, Binah is significantly upgraded by the influence of Chokhmah. The heart is often beset by conflicting emotions and crippling indecision. This conflict comes about because the right and left ventricles of the heart are the "seats" of the good and evil inclinations, respectively. As King Solomon explains (see *Ecclesiastes* 10:2), the right side of the heart represents man's conscience that leads him to do good deeds, while the left side of the heart connotes the base desires that try to lead a person astray.

For example, a person decides to go on a diet and lose weight. This is a decision of the mind, and may be a correct one. But if he starts to rationalize his resolve—for example, telling himself that it is too close to holiday time, when he will be hard-pressed to resist food and treats—he will usually change his decision. This is a common occurrence and reflects an inability to transform the potential into the actual.

By internalizing Chokhmah into Binah—that is, by approaching decisions using a blend of intellect and emotion—we can counteract any direct or indirect attack of the evil inclination and channel our potential into creative energy, as opposed to non-creative or destructive energy. When the mind (Chokhmah) and heart (Binah) work in harmony, our primal will (Keter) can manifest in a productive result, which becomes readily apparent in our Daat, the practical application of that knowledge.

Building a Sound Structure

"A house is built with wisdom and established with understanding; with knowledge, its rooms will be filled with precious treasures" (*Proverbs* 24:3-4).

To apply the ideas of Chokhmah, Binah and Daat to our goal—the "house," or end-product of our potential—we must first develop our Chokhmah (wisdom). Next, we will utilize Binah (understanding) to figure out how to keep that "house" secure and see to its maintenance. Still, it is only when we attain Daat (knowledge) that we fill its rooms with proper and tasteful furnishings. These furnishings are the practical knowledge that we apply daily to live a full and contented life.

Rebbe Nachman teaches that the first step in "building"—building a life, a marriage, a livelihood, etc.—is to use our intellect. To do so, we need focus. It all begins in the mind.

A person's very essence is his mind. Wherever a person's thoughts are, that is where he himself is—all of him. This explains why it is so important to avoid all bad thoughts. Otherwise, that is where your place will be. Force yourself to think good thoughts so that you will be worthy of knowing and understanding God. Then your place will be with Him; you will be merged with Him. The greater your perception of God, the more you will become merged with Him, and then you will achieve eternal life (*Likutey Moharan* I, 2:13).

The true essence of a person, what a person refers to as "I," is the soul (*Likutey Moharan* I, 22:5). Thus, at the very same time that we are developing our potential, we are also developing ourselves. This process is hidden from the casual observer, but one who sincerely seeks self-improvement and growth will merit to open up the gates of true self-knowledge.

> Everything in this world has some purpose; nothing is meaningless. Everything also has a root. A person may have no understanding of what is happening around him, but if he succeeds in just doing what God wants, it is very good, and he is fortunate indeed. He must ask God to help him know what He wants, and then do it—that, and only that. But when a person is worthy of receiving illumination and he comes to understand what he is accomplishing, that is even better. The very Heavens are opened for him. Wisdom opens up to him, and God will reveal to that person what he is really accomplishing (*Tzaddik* #92).

When God opens up for us the channels of wisdom and understanding, we become better equipped to handle life's challenges. Not only will we attain wisdom and understanding in and for this world, but we will also begin to experience the Future— what we call the World to Come—in the present. The delight of the World to Come stems from knowing, praising and thanking God, a delight that supersedes any other pleasure in this world (*Likutey Moharan* II, 2:1). However, the Talmud teaches (*Berakhot* 5a) that the World to Come (i.e., expanded knowledge) cannot be attained without suffering. In our context, this refers to the challenges we encounter when we attempt to advance our plans and concretize our thoughts. If we desire to accomplish, we must not shirk these challenges.

Rebbe Nachman notes that pain and suffering stem from a lack of understanding. Setbacks are not random occurrences, but specific challenges which God places in our path for our own good. They strengthen our desire for the goals we seek, or encourage us to overcome the difficulties and thereby receive more reward for our efforts. The Rebbe explains:

> If people feel they have problems and difficulties in life, or that they are lacking certain things that they need—be it sufficient

income, children, physical health or whatever—the reason for their feeling is that they lack true understanding. When understanding is perfect, nothing is lacking. The essence of the eternal life of the Future is bound up with the degree of understanding that will exist then. All will have knowledge of the Creator, and through this they will all be merged in His unity and live eternally, just as God does. It is through knowing Him that we become merged with Him—this is the main joy of the World to Come. For this reason you should be very careful to guard your thoughts in purity and holiness and to avoid any bad thoughts. Think only about Torah and devotion and constantly aim to achieve higher levels of perception of God. Everything depends on this (*Likutey Moharan* I, 21:12).

The prophet Isaiah describes the revelation that will flood the world in future times (*Isaiah* 11:6,9): "The wolf will dwell with the sheep and the leopard will lie down with the kid...for the world will be filled with knowledge of God." Then we will recite the blessing, "Who is good and Who does good," for everything (see *Pesachim* 50a), because everyone will know that there is really no bad in the world at all and that everything that each one of us is going through now is all for the good (*Likutey Moharan* I, 21:12). Having faced adversity and grown through it, what could the suffering have been if not good?

To know that everything that happens to you is for your own good is to have a foretaste of the World to Come. The way to come to this realization is through talking out your heart before a Torah scholar. Through this you will come to understand that everything that happens to you every day of your life is all for your good. Everything springs from the love God has for you. To be serene and patient regardless of what you encounter in life is the highest level of Daat, the knowledge and understanding of God. You must have faith that everything is for your ultimate good (*Likutey Moharan* I, 4:2-4).

This perspective also highlights our unique role on earth and our intrinsic self-worth. The creation of man was neither a cosmic accident nor an evolutionary quirk. Rather, God fashioned man at the very beginning to be the apex of Creation, and imbued him with the intelligence to recognize his Creator. Every thought and action that we perform according to our perceptions of God and life has incredible value in God's eyes.

As Rebbe Nachman puts it: "When a man goes like *this* with his hands, a movement like *this* takes place in all the worlds. And when he goes like *that* with his hands, a movement like *that* takes place in all the worlds." Furthermore: "If they turned a man inside out they would see that thousands upon thousands of worlds depend on every single sinew of his body" (*Tzaddik* #504-505).

All depends on man. And man can advance his own position by improving his perceptions of God. "The essence of knowledge (Daat) is to know God in your heart and not just in your mind," Rebbe Nachman explains. "You should bring the perceptions of God from your mind (Chokhmah) down to the next lower level, to your heart (Binah), and bind that knowledge of God to your heart until you are gripped by fear and awe of God's greatness and are awakened to truly serve Him. This way, you merit the highest level of fear, which is awe of God's exaltedness. Then you will know what awe is all about" (*Likutey Moharan* I, 15:3).

Memory Power

How do we become aware of our wisdom, to "know what we know"? The trick is to remember what we have learned and to keep it alive and active in our minds. Physiologists call this memory.

You must be very careful to cultivate a good memory and not fall into forgetfulness. What is a good memory? It means constantly keeping the thought of the World to Come [i.e., the goal] in the forefront of your mind and never forgetting about it. It would be a very good thing to make it a daily habit, as soon as you open your eyes in the morning and before you do anything else, to bring to mind that the World to Come is the only true goal. Do this as soon as you wake up. This is the concept of memory in general.

Follow this through into every detail of the day. Use every thought, word and deed which God sends you each day to broaden your understanding and perception of God. Understand that every one is a hint that God sends you in order to draw you closer to Him. God Himself is Infinite and without end. But He "contracts" Himself, as it were, to our level, using all the experiences that He sends us each day, in order to signal to us and guide us. It is up to us to recognize this and find the messages in all the thoughts, words and deeds that are sent to us, in order that we may reach a deeper insight and come closer to God (*Likutey Moharan* I, 54:2).

Keeping the World to Come in the forefront of our minds reminds us constantly of the big picture, of a goal that is worth pursuing. When we focus on that goal, we suddenly become more aware of all the tools that God has placed within our reach to aid us in our quest. Our natural surroundings, for example, will be transformed from casual contact into meaningful experiences, for God created all and dwells in its midst. We can marvel at a stunning sunset, or we can contemplate the awesomeness of the One Who created that sunset, binding our minds to God. This awareness can also spur us to reach beyond our limitations and develop the Godly potential that lies within.

We must be careful, though, not to overextend ourselves. Rebbe Nachman cautions us to proceed in every endeavor in a measured and orderly way. One who tries to overstep his intellectual level, either through speculation or by delving too deeply in esoteric wisdom without preparation, runs the risk of passing beyond the bounds of holiness into grave misunderstandings and other errors. As the Talmud states (*Chagigah* 13a), "That which is too wonderful for you, you must not search out" (*Likutey Moharan* I, 54:2).

The many pleasurable attractions of this world may also sidetrack us if we are not careful. The Rebbe once remarked:

The Evil Urge [i.e., the inclination to minimize or ignore that which is truly important] is like a prankster running through a crowd, showing his tightly closed hand. No one knows what he is holding. He goes up to each one and asks, "What do you suppose

I have in my hand?" Each one imagines that the closed hand contains just what he desires most. They all hurry and run after the prankster. Then, when he has tricked them all into following him, he opens his hand. It is completely empty.

The same is true of the Evil One. He fools the world, tricking it into following him. All men think that his hand contains what they desire. But in the end, he opens his hand. There is nothing in it, and no desire is ever fulfilled.

Worldly pleasures are like sunbeams in a dark room. They may actually seem solid, but one who tries to grasp a sunbeam finds nothing in his hand. The same is true of all worldly desires (Rabbi Nachman's Wisdom #6).

Let us also make good use of our time and not "kill time." Killing time translates into "killing" ourselves, because we have wasted a short span of our own lifetimes! For a project as important as developing ourselves, Rebbe Nachman urges us to consider the value of our days:

If we are perceptive, we will recognize that time in this world is really nothing. The sensation of time stems from deficient understanding. The greater our perception, the more we see that, in reality, time does not exist. We can actually feel how time flies like a passing shadow and a cloud that will soon disappear. If we take this to heart, we will be free of worries about mundane matters and will have the strength and determination to snatch what we can—a good deed here, a lesson there—in order to gain something truly enduring out of this life. We will then gain the life of the Eternal World, which is completely beyond time (Likutey Moharan I, 61).

When we apply our Chokhmah (wisdom) and utilize our Binah (understanding), we attain Daat, the full knowledge of what we want. From there, we can begin to actualize our desire. The Rebbe points out, "Daat—true knowledge—draws down God's lovingkindness" (Aleph-Bet Book, Sweetening Judgment, A34). When we draw Daat, we invoke the power of Keter (compassion) to mitigate the challenges that arise from the tzimtzum, making it easier for us to develop and grow.

To attain true levels of perception, we must also draw upon the Daat of the Tzaddikim. Tzaddikim are people who have succeeded in developing their potential and are able to impart their knowledge to others. "True wisdom," Rebbe Nachman explains, "is the wisdom of the Tzaddikim. Wisdom brings them to a lofty perception of God and gives them the power to communicate their perception to those who follow them. Compared with their wisdom, all other ideological systems are utter foolishness" (*Likutey Moharan* I, 30:1).

> The fact is that the Holy Torah and the true Tzaddikim radiate a great light throughout all the worlds, and their light is thousands and thousands of times greater than all of this world and its vanities. However, people are steeped in those vanities and this world appears most immediately to their vision. Therefore they imagine that there is nothing better than this world, although it is actually very small and of absolutely no substance or consequence whatsoever. Still, the small earth (that is, materialism) stands in front of their eyes and prevents them from seeing the great and holy light of the Torah and the Tzaddikim.
>
> It is as if you were to hold a small coin directly in front of your eye and, as a result, you were unable to see a large mountain—despite the fact that the mountain is thousands of times larger than the coin. Similarly, this world and the desire for wealth and more money stand in front of a person's eyes and prevent him from seeing the great light of the Torah and the Tzaddikim (ibid., 133).

It is not sufficient to attain perception only for oneself. Each person must develop his Daat and then pass it on to others, so that they too can experience the satisfaction of developing their potential. The growth of the world depends on it. Rebbe Nachman adds an even deeper insight: "A person must transmit his Daat to others so that even after he dies he can 'live on' through the Daat and perceptions he left behind in this world. This can be accomplished through one's children, and by teaching others" (*Likutey Moharan* II, 7:4).

All our good intentions contribute to bringing forth good into the world, good that lingers and that helps future generations to develop and bring forth even more good, forever and ever.

5

$\approx$

THE MIDOT
Overview

Each of us is gifted with a mind that reflects our will (Keter) as well as our overall intellect (Chokhmah, Binah and Daat). We also possess a "heart" (the alternative of Binah/Understanding, as above, p. 80), an emotional marvel that reacts according to the situations we encounter and to our own characters (thus, one can be said to have a "heart of gold," a "heart of stone," etc.). All our potential lies within our minds and hearts. Yet if it remains there, potent but undeveloped, it is valueless. What good is potential that goes nowhere? We must reach into our minds and hearts and process our potential, making the necessary strides to excel in life.

We also need to know how to *use* our potential. In our minds, we can do anything and everything—climb insurmountable mountains, plumb the depths of the sea, fly through the air. But real life isn't like that. We must work hard to sort out what is imagination or illusion from what is feasible and within reason. If something lies beyond our ability, we should recognize it and steer clear of it. Rebbe Nachman repeatedly warns against recklessness, extremism and fanaticism in any type of spiritual, physical, emotional or financial endeavor (see *Rabbi Nachman's Wisdom* #51).

The tools that will help us sort, examine and decide on a plan are the seven lower Sefirot. These seven Sefirot are called Midot (Attributes or Characteristics), and reflect the wide range of emotions and capabilities seen in the broad spectrum of humanity.

Sefirah	Translation	Concept	Human Parallel
Chesed	Lovingkindness	benevolences, giving	right arm/hand
Gevurah	Strength	judgment, restraint	left arm/hand
Tiferet	Beauty	truth, harmony	torso
Netzach	Everlasting	victory, endurance	right leg
Hod	Splendor	empathy, submission	left leg
Yesod	Foundation	covenant, channel	sexual organ
Malkhut	Kingship	authority, receiving, reciprocity	mouth, mate

Recall that each Sefirah acts as a filter for the one above it, working to devolve God's Light into lesser and lesser intensity. The energy of our own creative process, encapsulated in raw form in the upper Sefirot of Chokhmah, Binah and Daat, must be filtered down through the lower Sefirot of Chesed, Gevurah, Tiferet, Netzach, Hod, Yesod and Malkhut to bring our thoughts to fruition.

Say, for example, you have a burning urge to invent a certain type of computer program. You have thought through the design in your mind and sat down to outline the development process on paper. As trial and error brings each step closer to the finished product, each step of the "earlier, enlarged picture" is diminished, but more clearly defined. In the same way, each succeeding Sefirah diminishes the influx of the intensity of the upper Sefirot to bring forth a satisfactory outcome.

As discussed earlier (see p. 55), the energy that jump-starts the process lies in the principle of opposing forces. The Sefirot, in their ideal, "rectified" state, are arrayed in three columns: right, left and center (see also Appendix).

Left Column	Center Column	Right Column
Gevurah		Chesed
	Tiferet	
Hod		Netzach
	Yesod	
	Malkhut	

The right column always represents mercy, giving and kindness— it is characterized by unconditional love and acceptance, and a willingness to transcend boundaries through a merging of self and other. The left column always represents severity, discipline and restraint—it emphasizes obligations and responsibilities, defined boundaries and self-definition. While each column alone might seem to have nothing at all to do with the other, in truth, they are complementary opposites. This relationship is actualized in the center column. Harmony is achieved when we learn to balance the opposing aspects of our personalities. The center column synthesizes the seemingly opposing forces of "right" and "left," bringing about harmony, unity and peace.

We see the same principle at work when we consider how the Sefirot parallel human physiology. Note that Chesed represents the right arm/hand, Gevurah the left arm/hand, and Tiferet the torso. Just as the torso acts as the fulcrum for the opposing sides of the body, Tiferet balances the extreme tendencies of the "right" and "left" sides of our personalities. Similarly, Netzach represents the right leg, Hod the left leg, and Yesod the sexual organ between them. Netzach corresponds to the impetus to move forward, Hod to remaining grounded, and Yesod to basing all momentum on a foundation of morality and righteousness.

With both our hands and our legs, we draw things towards us—symbolizing acceptance and giving—or push them away from us—symbolizing rejection and disassociation. The torso and the pelvic region, which contain the spinal cord and backbone, imply the courage to stand upright and be strong in our convictions. Thus, our body language reveals much about the ideas we have been developing within the inner recesses of our minds, and empowers us to start bringing those ideas to fruition.

The Kabbalah also teaches that when we use the power vested in us beneficially, for our own good as well as that of our friends, neighbors, communities and environment, our conduct directly influences Divine Providence. We have the ability to reach out towards God and bring His blessings down to earth.

6

≈≋≈

CHESED
The Light of Love and Joy

The word Chesed translates as lovingkindness, but it means much more than that. Chesed represents an overwhelming desire to give—and keep giving continuously—no matter what the other person has done, or even whether he or she deserves it. Chesed manifests as unrestricted love between fellow human beings, as well as the benevolences that God showers upon man.

Chesed also encompasses joy. One who makes use of his intellectual abilities and has set out in a good direction will feel positive and happy about his prospects. A joyous attitude leads to success in any endeavor. Empirically, we see that a person who performs chesed for others naturally feels a sense of joy and fulfillment due to his acts of kindness. Simply put, making others happy is a major contributor to personal happiness.

Chesed also represents hope—hope for a successful conclusion to our efforts, hope for additional success, and hope for a better future. Therefore, this Sefirah signifies the fact that hope always exists.

The fact that Chesed is the first of the lower Sefirot to receive the energy of the upper Sefirot indicates that our first concrete step to realizing our potential must be established on love and geared towards bringing forth benevolent results. We should intentionally focus our thoughts on doing the right thing, and on having the result affect ourselves and others in a beneficial manner. Included in this idea is the giving of charity, an act that represents selflessness and connection to others. As Rebbe Nachman teaches, "All the charity and kindness that you do in this world creates Heavenly advocates and produces great harmony between you and your Father in Heaven" (*Aleph-Bet Book, Tzedakah,* A1).

Obviously, to acquire the attribute of Chesed, we must *do* acts of Chesed. We must perform them as best as we can, whether with our bodies (by physically assisting others), with our emotions (by listening to and caring for others), or with our possessions (by lending equipment, sharing our time and, of course, giving charity). Giving advice to others is also an aspect of Chesed, especially when we make an effort to understand the other person's problem and counsel accordingly. If we're not capable of dispensing proper advice, we should refrain from doing so; it is also Chesed not to mislead anyone.

Rebbe Nachman offers these guidelines for acquiring and developing the attribute of Chesed:

> Learn the Thirteen Divine Attributes of Lovingkindness (cf. *Exodus* 34:6-7) in order to fulfill them in practice. Cultivate the quality of love and do as many kindnesses as you can for other people. When you strive to fulfill each of the Thirteen Attributes of Love, the Thirteen Supernal Attributes of Love are aroused, and destructive angels brought into being through sin are humbled. Our own acts of kindness arouse God's forgiveness, and He passes over our sins, one after the other (*Rabbi Nachman's Wisdom* #89).

"Sins" signify our errors and mistakes, misdeeds and transgressions. It's easy to fall into a rut of depression when we look back at the wrongful things we did and see how much personal misery and suffering they caused, not to mention how much they hurt the people we feel close to. Depression also engenders self-centeredness and ego-sensitivity—the opposite of humility. When we chastise ourselves—"I hate myself for doing that, I hate this, I hate that..."—we arouse negative feelings that tend to depress us further and suppress our potential for good. Rebbe Nachman says that focusing on the "wrong" connects us to "wrong." To develop properly, we must focus on the good. By seeking good, by *actively* searching for love and kindness, we develop an affinity for those characteristics. Then love, benevolence, kindness and joy become an integral part of our lives.

> Know! In this world you must pass over a very narrow bridge. The main thing is not to be afraid at all. Fortify and cheer yourself greatly both by finding some merit and good point in yourself—since how is it possible that you never did anything good in your life?—and by the fact that God did not make you a heathen. Dance and skip in order to come to joy, until through this joy you will merit to return to God (*Likutey Moharan* II, 48).

Seeking out and emphasizing the good within ourselves is one of Rebbe Nachman's key teachings. By finding good, by thinking positive, we can focus. When we despair of our misdeeds and begin to think of them as our essence, we lose the ability to focus even on what we did wrong! By engaging in the positive we can ascend above the "wrong," bringing the light of love, kindness and joy into our lives.

In one of his most important lessons on this subject, the Rebbe exhorts us to search out the good points in ourselves and others. "By finding some merit and good in yourself, you can actually effect a shift from a 'guilty verdict' to a favorable judgment, and you will then be able to return to God," he says. "With this approach, you can inspire and cheer yourself and be able to pray, sing and give thanks to God. This pathway is an indispensable foundation if you really want to draw close to God and not waste your life. The most important thing is to distance yourself from sadness and depression and not become discouraged" (*Likutey Moharan* I, 282).

Depression, the Rebbe explains, is really another word for despair and hopelessness. When a person is depressed, his intellect and mind go into exile. This makes it very hard for him to concentrate on any goal, much less that of coming close to and experiencing God. When someone feels happy, in contrast, his mind becomes settled and he is able to understand things clearly. Joy is freedom—it frees the intellect from its exile. One can control his mind and intellect in any way he desires so he can concentrate on his goal and return to God (*Likutey Moharan* II, 10).

Reb Noson observes that the Rebbe's writings are filled with all kinds of ways to stay happy, no matter what the situation. Even when a person is under great pressure, materially or spiritually, he can still discover ways to be happy, knowing that God will never abandon him. And if he can summon a little happiness under pressure, surely he will be downright joyous when God sends some respite from his difficulties (*Tzaddik* #593).

"Try to turn the sadness and depression and difficulties themselves into a reason for being happy," Rebbe Nachman suggests. "Say, 'Even though I'm the way I am, nevertheless I still have the merit of being Jewish. How many mitzvot do I carry out each day—saying the Shma, giving charity, etc.? Perhaps the way I perform the mitzvot leaves much to be desired. Even so, they still contain many good points, and in the upper worlds they bring great joy.' As long as you still go under the name of Israel, God takes great pride in you, as it is written (*Isaiah* 49:3), 'Israel, in whom I take pride'" (*Tzaddik* #593).

If we really set our minds to it, we will indeed find that amidst the worst troubles and suffering, there is still an opening through which we can convert all our depression into joy. The definition of true joy is when we drag out our darkness and depression against their will, forcing them to turn into happiness (*Likutey Moharan* II, 23).

A joyous person can express love; a positive person can confront even a monumental task without feeling overwhelmed by it. A cheerful person is willingly benevolent, spreading goodwill and kindness. Joy helps a person maintain a positive frame of mind, stay committed to the goal, and be energized towards success.

Joy also saves from sin. "Depression and anxiety are the main cause of sexual immorality. The foundation of the covenant lies in joy" (Likutey Moharan I, 169).[9] Being content in all areas of life—especially in the area of moral living—is a major task and accomplishment. "Sure, not everything is the way I want it. I want more—a better life, a greater sense of achievement. But for right now, I'm happy and satisfied." Be content with just as much as you need to take from this world. Rebbe Nachman adds that the effect of this contentment brings about a great unification in the upper worlds, releasing abundant blessings upon our world (Likutey Moharan I, 54:3).

Joy is not something that we should wait to happen. It is absolutely necessary to search for it and seek it out, even to force ourselves to become joyous.

> It is a great mitzvah to be happy at all times. Be determined to keep away from depression and aim to be happy constantly. Happiness is the remedy for all kinds of disease—because many illnesses are caused by depression. Be resourceful in order to make yourself happy. Often you must do something a little bit crazy in order to make yourself happy (Likutey Moharan II, 24).

Once Rebbe Nachman observed that it seems impossible to achieve happiness without some measure of foolishness (Rabbi Nachman's Wisdom #20). Owing to the many physical, emotional and financial troubles that each of us endures, the only way we can cheer ourselves may be by acting foolishly (Likutey Moharan II, 10). I know someone who would see children playing hopscotch on a sidewalk and jump the squares from one end to the other as he passed them by. Everyone would laugh. The children delighted in seeing an older man playing their game, and the man enjoyed making them smile—as well as being able to laugh at himself and thereby bring some joy into his life.

Music is another effective vehicle for increasing joy. Rebbe Nachman teaches that listening to and playing musical instruments actually leads to prophecy (which can only be achieved in a joyous frame of mind), as we find in Scripture (see II Kings 3:15).

---

[9] This idea will be discussed in greater detail in Chapter 9, below, where we discuss the energy of Yesod.

The Rebbe explains that there are two types of *ruach* (spirit or wind)—a gloomy (i.e., evil) ruach (*I Samuel* 16:14) and a good ruach (*Psalms* 143:10). The latter is the spirit of prophecy. Most people have both gloomy and joyous spirits, but they are intertwined. To draw out the good spirit, the musician moves his hands or breath across the instrument, shifting the air and thereby sifting the good ruach from the bad. The musician then finds and gathers the components of the good ruach to build the tune, which in turn develops the joyous spirit within the musician and the listener (see *Likutey Moharan* I, 54:7). Of course, not everyone can play music, nor is every person musically inclined. Still, the experience of hearing a nice piece of music almost always has the power to calm a person and lighten his mood.

Another way to master the state of joy is to constantly direct your thoughts towards the Source of all goodness. By contemplating this Source, everything that is good and joyous will be merged into one and radiate with abundant light (*Likutey Moharan* II, 34).

> Joy will also embolden you to take the necessary steps and have the courage of your convictions, despite people's opposition to your stand or efforts. For the main source of a person's boldness and unremitting determination to draw close to God's service is happiness and joy, as in the verse (*Nehemiah* 8:10), "Rejoicing in God is our strength, our boldness!" (*Likutey Moharan* I, 22:4).

Joy is a major factor in any endeavor, especially one as important as developing our potential. This is because Chesed immediately follows Binah, which parallels the heart. Most people will not pursue a goal that leads to sadness; rather, they will fill their hearts with excitement and enthusiasm for a positive outcome. Rebbe Nachman sums it up this way:

> The main source of joy is from the mitzvot, and joy is felt primarily in the heart. To whatever degree a person understands in his heart the greatness of the Creator, His Oneness and His Eternally Blessed Unity, so it is appropriate that he should rejoice over each and every mitzvah he performs, by which he merits to carry out the Will of God (*Likutey Moharan* I, 30:5).

By investing all our efforts with joy, we can bring ourselves into direct contact with our Creator in a most powerful way. This "contact" is actually what allows us to draw upon the Creator's energies—powers far greater than our own. Joy allows us to reach beyond our personal limitations to develop an even greater potential and attain greater goals. The ARI himself said that he attained his awesome levels of Kabbalah-understanding specifically because of his joy when performing the mitzvot (see *Mishnah Berurah* 669:11; *Pri Etz Chaim, Shaar HaLulav,* Chapter 8). Joy allows our natural tendencies towards love, kindness and benevolence to blossom, and brings out our very best.

Dealing With Sadness and Pain

Obviously, it is difficult to feel joyous at all times. The vicissitudes of life don't allow us that pleasure. Therefore, as an "extension" of joy, we are allowed to feel "brokenhearted." Rebbe Nachman explains:

> Heartbreak is in no way related to sadness and depression. Depression comes from the Other Side and is hated by God. But a broken heart over one's distance from God is very dear and precious to God. For the average person, brokenheartedness can easily degenerate into depression. You should therefore set aside some time each day for heartbreak. You should isolate yourself with a broken heart before God for a given time. But the rest of the day should be joyful (*Likutey Moharan* II, 24).

> The Rebbe emphasized this many times, telling us not to be brokenhearted except for a fixed time each day. He said that we should always be joyful and never depressed. Depression is like anger and rage. It is like a complaint against God for not fulfilling one's wishes. But a person with a broken heart is like a child pleading before his father. He is like a baby crying and complaining because his father is far away (*Rabbi Nachman's Wisdom* #41-42).

It's natural to experience sadness or pain. But it's what you do with your heart that determines where it will take you. Rebbe Nachman suggests that you take your pain and transform it into prayer before God, creating a channel for that negative energy to be released in a positive form.[10]

Prayer and Torah study can help us tap directly into the positive energy of Chesed. "True prayer should be filled with the quality of love," Rebbe Nachman advises. "Prayer is a plea for God's grace and kindness. The ability to love depends on understanding. When the strength of love is sapped, anger and cruelty come in its place and understanding diminishes" (Likutey Moharan II, 8).

Regarding Torah study, the Rebbe teaches: "Anger and unkindness arise when people's understanding is limited. The deeper their understanding, the more their anger disappears and kindness, love and peace spread. This is why the study of Torah, which deepens understanding, brings love and peace into the world and banishes anger" (Likutey Moharan I, 56:1-3). Further: "If you are joyous, it will bring you to new horizons in Torah. Joy is a vessel with which to draw upon the wellsprings of the Torah's vitality and freshness" (ibid., 65).

According to Rebbe Nachman, Torah study and prayer actualize the love that was in potentia between the Jewish People and their Father in Heaven before Creation, when the Jewish People still existed only in God's Mind, so to speak. This love is beyond time and is identified with the deep inner meaning of the Torah. It transcends every wrongdoing, every bias and all anger, producing a world of love, peace and joy (Likutey Moharan I, 33). Therefore Rebbe Nachman recommends:

> Pray with great joy, even if this happiness is forced. Happiness is always a virtue, especially during prayer. If you are disturbed and unhappy, you can at least put on a happy front. Deep down you may be depressed, but if you act in a happy way, you will eventually be worthy of true joy. This is true of every holy thing. If you have no enthusiasm, put on a front. Act enthusiastically and the feeling will eventually become genuine (Rabbi Nachman's Wisdom #74).

---

[10] This idea will be developed in greater detail in Chapter 10, below, where we discuss the energy of Malkhut.

DON'T WORRY, BE HAPPY!

Rebbe Nachman expressed the rewards of positive thinking in a memorable parable:

There was once a poor man who earned a living by digging clay and selling it. Once, while digging, he discovered a diamond that was obviously worth a great deal. He took it to an expert to ascertain its value. The expert said, "No one here will be able to afford such a jewel. Go to London, the capital, and there you will be able to sell it."

The man was so poor he could not afford to make the journey. He sold everything he had and went from door to door, collecting funds for the trip. Finally he had enough to take him as far as the sea. He then wanted to board a ship, but he did not have any money. He approached the captain of one of the ships and showed him his diamond. The captain immediately welcomed him aboard the ship with great honor, assuming that he was a very wealthy and trustworthy person. He gave the poor man a first-class cabin and treated him like a wealthy personage.

The poor man's cabin had a view of the sea. Every day he sat by his porthole, looking at his diamond and rejoicing. He was especially particular to admire his diamond during mealtimes, since eating in good spirits is highly beneficial for digestion.

One day, he sat down to eat with the diamond lying in front of him on the table, where he could see it and enjoy it. Sitting there, he dozed off. Meanwhile, the mess boy came and cleared off the table, shaking the tablecloth with its crumbs and the diamond into the sea. When the poor man awoke and realized what had happened, he almost went mad with grief. He knew the captain was a ruthless man who would not hesitate to kill him for his fare.

Having no other choice, he continued to act happy, as if nothing had happened. The captain would usually speak to him a few hours every day, and on this day, he put himself in good spirits, so that the captain was not aware that anything was wrong.

The captain said to him, "I want to buy a large quantity of wheat and I will be able to sell it in London for a huge profit. But I am afraid that I will be accused of stealing from the king's treasury. Therefore, I will arrange for the wheat to be bought in your name. I will pay you well for your trouble."

The poor man agreed. As soon as they arrived in London, the captain died. The entire shipload of wheat was in the poor man's name, and it was worth many times more than the diamond.

Rabbi Nachman concluded: "The diamond did not belong to the poor man, and the proof is that he did not keep it. The wheat, however, did belong to him, and the proof is that he kept it. But he got what he deserved only because he remained positive" (*Rabbi Nachman's Stories, Parable #19*).

This parable accentuates the power of maintaining a positive attitude at all times. Additionally, when we integrate joy into our lives, we can attain great things—things we might have thought were out of our reach—just as the poor man became a wealthy man thanks to his positive frame of mind.

Giving Charity

Since Chesed is an expression of benevolence, it is fitting to conclude our discussion of this Sefirah with some ideas about charity.

Charity has several meanings. It usually implies a financial gift, but it can also mean a kind word or a charitable act. Examples of the latter include looking for one's own good points, as well as judging others favorably. When Rebbe Nachman speaks about "giving charity," he refers to the range of Chesed opportunities that allow us to give of our time and our emotions as well as our possessions.

Give to charity before you pray. This is the way to avoid extraneous thoughts which come to you while praying. You will be able to pray properly without straying to the right or the left. You will order and measure your words on the scale of justice (*Likutey Moharan* I, 2).

Through giving charity and exercising the energy of Chesed, we can control our words and use them judiciously and meritoriously, bringing about blessing and beneficence.

How can we make our charity really count? Does it depend on how much we give, or how often? The truth is that giving charity is one thing, but giving where it really helps spells the difference. Saving the rain forests or protecting the whales, tigers, minks and skunks benefit the environment, but no gift is greater than charity to other people. In a fascinating twist on giving, Rebbe Nachman reveals that the benefits of supporting a certain type of recipient can pay back dividends that benefit all mankind, increasing the amount of love and joy in the world:

> When you give charity to the true Tzaddikim and to their followers who genuinely deserve it, it is as if you gave charity to many, many Jewish souls (*Likutey Moharan* I, 17:6).

Each Tzaddik is inclusive of the many souls that he leads and directs. The charity he receives allows him to continue to direct and benefit others. Thus, giving charity to a Tzaddik is equivalent to giving to many people.

With such powerful consequences at stake, it stands to reason that giving charity is not always easy. We may be reluctant to part with our "hard-earned cash," or be tempted to evaluate the real need of the recipient and conclude that giving less is just as acceptable as giving more. Our main goal in giving charity, Rebbe Nachman teaches, is to "break our instinct to be cruel and to turn it into lovingkindness, so that we give generously. Charity has the power to widen the entrance to all areas in which we need to proceed. When we want to embark upon a certain path—a new job, a new relationship, a new home; indeed, any new beginning—we first need to make an opening in order to enter our new path. This is why all beginnings are hard. Giving charity opens that entrance and even expands it, so we can embark on our new path to further develop our potential" (*Likutey Moharan* II, 4:2).

Miserliness and the desire to hold onto one's money reflect "the face of the Other Side," the Rebbe adds.

> Those who fall prey to the desire for money and who do not believe that the Blessed Holy One can sustain a person with only a small amount of effort on the person's part; who chase after their livelihood with enormous effort; who "eat their bread in sadness"; and who are replete with downheartedness and depression—these people are attached to the face of the Other Side, to the dark face, to sadness, depression and death.

> On the other hand, people who conduct their business with faith and who prevail in their own minds to be happy with their portion; who truly know and believe with perfect faith that livelihood and wealth come only from God, but that God simply wants them to make some small effort for their livelihood—these people cleave to the light of the face of holiness, to the radiant face which is life and joy (*Likutey Moharan* I, 23:1).

7

❧

GEVURAH
The Light of Boundaries

We have seen that Chesed represents giving. What happens, though, if the beneficence is too much and cannot be handled properly by the beneficiary? What if unrestricted love becomes overbearing? Can Chesed still be called kindness? Is there a way to stop Chesed from being overwhelming? The answer lies in the next Sefirah, Gevurah.

Gevurah means strength, power, heroism or courage. It implies great power and energy, along with willpower and toughness. It is the "left hand" to Chesed's "right hand," the discipline and restraint to Chesed's benevolence and beneficence. Gevurah acts to restrain the overwhelming attributes associated with Chesed, allowing us to define, contain and properly utilize the blessings found in the latter Sefirah.

In the Kabbalah, Gevurah serves as the attribute of Judgment, because a judgment imposes restraining or constricting orders with regard to a person's movements. One who must pay a fine for misbehavior or who is sent to prison for a crime is no longer free to act as he wishes. On a deeper level, Gevurah represents "severities"—harsh suffering that results when a judgment is not tempered with compassion. (For example, the original restrictions placed upon a person are considered too lenient and when the case is reviewed, a harsher sentence is handed down.)

Gevurah, in a negative sense, can also be associated with anger. Rebbe Nachman teaches that when a person is angry, he is said to be in a state of "constricted intellect" (see *Likutey Moharan* I, 21:12). An angry person often acts as if he is "blinded" by rage and will rarely listen to reason; hence, anger constricts his intellect. All these ideas of constriction are seen in the concept of Gevurah, which is also, conceptually, the Tzimtzum of Creation.

Gevurah emphasizes our responsibilities even—and especially— while we are engaged in acts of Chesed. It fortifies us with the discipline necessary to constrain the overwhelming desires of our minds and hearts, and to establish parameters to surround and protect our efforts to actualize our potential. It gives us the power to control our natural inclinations and desires, a necessary trait in all areas of life.

Included within the boundaries of Gevurah is the conscious avoidance of anger, jealousy and any form of cruelty. For example, a parent might wish to discipline a child. Is the discipline a result of the parent's desire for the child's welfare, or his own impatience? Alternately, in the area of heroism, are one's efforts solely dedicated to God and Godliness, or do his intentions lean towards self-aggrandizement and one-upmanship? Gevurah—restraint— demands that we continually evaluate our thoughts, words and deeds and purge them of ulterior motives and hidden agendas.

Gevurah also implies acting with simplicity. A self-disciplined person approaches each task in a simple and straightforward manner. A person who acts in a sophisticated manner, constantly reaching beyond his capabilities or the task at hand, will soon find himself treading in deep water. Philosophical pursuits of the intellect, for example, steer a person away from God and Godliness and the attainment of his rightful goals.

By invoking Gevurah in the proper manner, we can enhance our lives and become true recipients of the blessings and bounty brought down through Chesed and the Mochin. Moreover, when we properly invoke the power of Gevurah in our own lives, we can "convince" God, as it were, to restrain His judgments, which in turn allows us to benefit from His Chesed.

Let us turn to Rebbe Nachman for advice on acquiring and developing this invaluable attribute.

> Always remember you are a part of God above. The essence of Godliness is to be found in the heart. The Godliness in your heart is infinite. There is no end to the light of the flame that burns there. The holy desire which is there is infinite. But this same burning passion makes it impossible for you to accomplish anything at all in your service of God, nor would you be able to reveal any good trait, if you did not hold this passion within certain limits. You must "contract" it, so to speak, in order to be able to serve God in a measured and orderly way. God desires your service. There are specific actions and devotions which He asks of you. He wants you to develop your character traits and behavior in an orderly, systematic manner. This is how His kingship will be revealed (*Likutey Moharan* I, 49:1).

The passion about which Rebbe Nachman speaks is holy desire taken to the wrong extreme. Most of us are more familiar with the opposite type of passion, that of our evil inclination. This is a burning desire to go against the Will of God—to be lazy, uncaring, mean, hardhearted, and all the other adjectives that pose a challenge to God and His world. If we let our evil inclination burn without restraint, our lives will be totally subjugated to the negative traits and immoral attractions of this world.

But one who subdues his evil inclination must make sure he doesn't go too far to the other extreme. Zealousness and fanaticism have no place in Rebbe Nachman's code; they represent a force of "unrestrained love" beyond one's control. They act to occlude God's Kingship, not reveal it.

Rebbe Nachman is not the only teacher who advocates self-control, but his path offers the most simplified approach to mastering it. He expresses it this way: "Free choice is really that simple. If you want, you do it. If you don't want, you don't do it!" (*Likutey Moharan* II, 110). Reb Noson adds that he recorded this statement because of its towering significance. Many people think they do not have control over themselves. They are steeped in their habits from early on and feel they cannot exercise any restraint. But this is not true. At all times, in all places, a person has free choice. "If you want, you do it. If not, not!"

This leads to another important idea: We can only invoke our Gevurah if we believe we have that strength within us. Faith in ourselves is the prerequisite for tapping into the energy of this Sefirah. It takes enormous strength to maintain our beliefs and act upon them when necessary. This manifestation of faith is the manifestation of Gevurah, resulting in both control of a situation that we believe is for our good and self-control, as we utilize our energies to move in the direction that is *really* the right choice for us. None of this can be accomplished except through the simplified approach, as Rebbe Nachman teaches, "The greatest cleverness is to work out how to avoid sophistication" (*Likutey Moharan* II, 44).

"Many times the Rebbe said that no sophistication is needed in serving God," Reb Noson adds. "All that is required is simplicity, sincerity and faith" (*Rabbi Nachman's Wisdom* #101).

Thought-Control

Of all the areas under our control, it seems that the mind often "has a mind of its own." Rebbe Nachman notes that the mind is the training ground for Gevurah and self-control:

> Be very careful to guard your mind and your thoughts and make sure that you never admit to alien ideas or ways of looking at things. All problems and sins come from abusing the sanctity of the mind by admitting alien thoughts and ideologies. To achieve true repentance and to make amends for all one's sins, it is necessary to cleanse the mind of all these alien ideas. Wisdom and intelligence are actually the soul. By clearing the mind of alien ideologies, the faculty of thought is elevated to its Source. This is the essence of returning to God (*Likutey Moharan* I, 35:1).

It's especially difficult to control our thoughts during prayer. It sounds so simple to spend a few minutes with a siddur, or to pour out our hearts to the Master of the World, but it is far from easy to combat the deluge of thoughts, fantasies, memories, to-do lists and other distractions that bombard us right at that quiet moment. What's worse, the very act of trying to rid ourselves of these thoughts makes them entrench themselves deeper.

Surprising but true: "The best way to deal with [unwanted thoughts] is simply to ignore them," Rebbe Nachman teaches. "Act as if you were completely unconcerned. Refuse to listen. Carry on with what you are doing—studying, praying, working, etc. Pay no attention to the thoughts or fantasies at all. Don't keep looking around to see if they have gone away. Just carry on with what you are trying to do. In the end, they will go away of their own accord. But you should understand that this method is only a temporary measure. In the long run, your task is to sanctify and purify your body. To achieve this you must go to the Tzaddikim to learn the paths of truth. Then thoughts like these will disappear completely" (*Likutey Moharan* I, 72).

Is it really possible to control our thoughts? Rebbe Nachman assures us that it is. He compares thought to a wayward horse that has turned away from the path and is trying to head off in the wrong direction. The rider need only pull on the bridle to force the horse back onto the path. In the same way, a person's thoughts are completely under his control (*Likutey Moharan* II, 50).

Thought-control doesn't happen overnight. But when we exercise self-control as often as possible, we learn that we *can* do it. We can also use to our advantage the fact that the mind cannot hold two thoughts at the same time. No matter what we're thinking about, the minute we introduce a new thought, the previous thought disappears automatically. Any thought can dislodge another— including thoughts about God and Torah and even about work and daily interests (*Likutey Moharan* I, 233).

Admittedly, the battle of the mind, between good and bad thoughts, rages all day long. What will happen if we don't exercise the control that's demanded of us and from time to time let our imaginations stroll off the straight and narrow? Rebbe Nachman has already anticipated this question, and provides the answer:

> When a person admits unholy thoughts to his mind, the holiness of his mind is reduced in direct proportion to the space occupied by these degraded thoughts. If you stick a pole into a riverbed, all kinds of dirt and filth gather around it. In the same way, all kinds of bad characteristics develop because of these unholy ideas, and the mind is assailed with desires and temptations. In fact, all the sins a person commits are ultimately caused by the unholy ideas he originally admitted to his mind. To achieve a pure mind, you must rid your mind of these thoughts. The mind is the soul, and when a person sanctifies his mind he purifies his soul, he merits to elevate everything to its root [the source of his potential] (*Likutey Moharan* I, 35:1).

Even if a person has been unsuccessful at controlling his thoughts for a long time, all is not lost. Every effort he does make to stem the tide will add a little more strength and a little more purity to his mind.

> A person can't always stop bad thoughts from entering his mind in the first place. But he does have the power to reject them once he becomes conscious of them. This is something very important, because it is the way to make amends for sins he may have committed earlier in his life. Perfect repentance has to balance the original sins exactly, and this is literally what happens here. Before, when he sinned, it was because the temptation entered his mind and he succumbed to it. Now the thought is in his mind again, but this time he rejects it (cf. *Likutey Moharan* I, 26).

So don't feel discouraged if you find all kinds of temptations and fantasies continually pressing on your mind. They are actually providing you with the opportunity to repent and make amends for the damage done in the past. *Today* you have the power to master your thoughts and temptations. When you do so, the sparks of holiness that shattered and fell because of your earlier transgressions are released, and you are able to purify yourself. Your mind and your voice will be purified and you will find harmony and peace. This peace can bring the whole world back to the service of God.

Keep It Simple

Let's see how our potential is developing. We had a good thought, it seemed that we could accomplish that idea, and we felt an overwhelming urge to start moving in the chosen direction. Unrestrained, however, we will never get beyond the desire to do what we want, and won't focus on the goal. How many of us look into the distance and set our sights on a certain objective? If we don't check our movements every step of the way, we can easily lose sight of our goal and even veer off course. The overwhelming Chesed that descends to us will be diverted and go to waste. By exercising Gevurah, we can restrain our enthusiasm from time to time and take the opportunity to re-examine the feasibility of our goals. Gevurah will also keep us from getting distracted.

Keeping things simple is the key to staying on track and on target. Sophistication, after all, requires knowledge of many things and takes them all into consideration when seeking a solution. However necessary it is to see the "whole picture," when it comes down to making a decision, a yes or no answer will really suffice. Gevurah (judgment and restraint) keeps us focused on the goal. Rebbe Nachman elaborates:

> Someone who follows his own ideas can easily fall into all kinds of traps and get into serious trouble. Too many people have been led astray by their own wisdom. They themselves have sinned and have caused many others to sin as well, all because of their fallacious "wisdom." The essence of the Jewish religion is to follow the path of purity and simplicity without sophistication—simply to make sure that God is present in everything you do. Have no thought at all for your own honor and glory. The only question is whether God's glory will be enhanced. If so, do it. If not, then don't do it. This way, you will never stumble (*Likutey Moharan* II, 12).

This teaching is based on one of Rebbe Nachman's most awesome lessons, "*Ayeh?*" This lesson was given in response to the impact of the *Haskalah* (Enlightenment movement) on the average Jew back in the late 1700s and early 1800s. Oppression by the Russian czars was suffocating the Jews at that time, and a new group of Jewish freethinkers arose that sought relief by abandoning the time-tested paths of Torah and prayer in favor of aping the surrounding culture. This effort, like other breakaway movements throughout the 1,700 years of Jewish exile that preceded it, only brought about new, sophisticated means of oppression, not to mention widespread assimilation.

Obviously, Rebbe Nachman's statement, "Too many people have been led astray by their own wisdom," does not refer to someone who uses his mind to seek solutions to problems. Why else was a person given a mind, if not to think?! Instead, the Rebbe is stressing the importance of simplicity. We have a path that works: the Torah. It has held us together as a Jewish nation for millennia. Why look for some new, convoluted path that *always* proves its inability to sustain and nourish the soul, the potential of the nation? Keep it simple. Keep focused on the goal. The true goal is the World to Come, but even in this world, the goals we seek are attainable if we but focus and concentrate on them with a simple approach.

> Serve God with simplicity and purity, pursuing no sophistication at all. This is the true goal. Never so much as open a book of philosophy. This is no part of the heritage of Jacob. All speculative philosophy contains the stumbling block of Amalek,[11] which is calculated to make people fall. In one moment they can lose worlds. There is no greater evil.
>
> Even books written by Jews which discuss speculative philosophy should be left alone, because they can harm the holy faith which is the root of everything. Thank God, we have many holy books today that are filled with sound guidance and the fear of God and are free of all speculation derived from the so-called "wisdom" of the Greeks. They are firmly founded on the holy words of the Sages of the Talmud and the Midrash. In particular, there are the books [of the Kabbalah] based on the teachings of Rabbi Shimon

---

[11] Archenemy of the Jewish People (c.f. *Deuteronomy* 25:17-19),

bar Yochai. Explore them and go through them again and again (*Likutey Moharan* II, 19).

Reb Noson explains, "The reason why the Rebbe forbade us to read even the philosophical works that are unimpeachable on religious grounds is because they raise very difficult questions about the ways of God and go into them at length—but when they come to answer them, the explanations they give are very weak and easily pulled down. Anyone who studies these works and tries to answer the questions rationally can be led to atheism when he realizes later on that the explanation is completely inadequate, while the problem continues to trouble him.

"The Rebbe told us to rely only on faith. If someone finds he has questions about such matters, he should know that it is impossible to give any explanations, because with our human minds it is impossible to comprehend the ways of God. All we have is faith—we must believe that everything is certainly correct and right, only with our minds it is impossible to understand God's ways" (*Tzaddik* #150).

The Rebbe once laughed and said: "If they would allow one dead soul to visit an assembly of philosophers, that would be the end of all their teachings!" (*Rabbi Nachman's Wisdom* #226).

When we marry action to decision, our commitment to avoid sophistication and errant philosophies will be successful.

> Rebbe Nachman said: "I have a great longing to institute a rule that each person study a fixed amount in our sacred literature each day without fail." He said that this should apply to those who are very far from holiness, even those who are caught in the evil trap and sin habitually, Heaven forbid. Still, the strength of the Torah is so great that it can free them from their habitual sins. If even the worst sinner would take upon himself a set practice to study a fixed amount every day, he would be able to escape from the evil trap. The Torah's strength is so great that it can accomplish everything. A person's main goal should be to do good and serve God without sophistication. Every good and holy thing can be done with absolute simplicity. One can study much Torah, do much good, and spend much time in prayer, all without sophistication at all (*Rabbi Nachman's Wisdom* #19).

THE SIMPLE MAN'S REWARD

Rebbe Nachman once said that God wins battles because of the simple folk who recite psalms with sincerity, and not because of those who use sophisticated means. He related this parable as an illustration:

A king once went hunting disguised as a simple man so that he would have freedom of movement. Suddenly a heavy rain began to fall, literally like a flood. His ministers scattered in all directions, and the king was in great danger. He searched until he found the house of a villager. The villager invited the king in and offered him some groats. He lit the stove and let the king sleep on his pallet.

This was very sweet and pleasant for the king. He was so tired and exhausted that it seemed as if he had never had such a pleasurable experience.

Meanwhile, the royal ministers searched high and low for the king, until they found him in this house. They wanted him to return to the palace with them. But the king said, "You did not even attempt to rescue me. Each one of you ran to save himself. But this man rescued me. Here I had the sweetest experience. Therefore, he will bring me back in his wagon, in these clothes, and he will sit with me on my throne" (*Rabbi Nachman's Stories, Parable #21*).

Before the coming of the Mashiach, Rebbe Nachman explains, the world will be flooded by atheism and immorality. This "flood" will come with such strength that it will even affect virtuous hearts, and no one will be able to fight it with any form of sophistication. All the "royal ministers" and leaders will be scattered, and the entire kingdom will not stand firm on its foundations. The only ones who will uphold God's Kingdom will be the Jews who recite psalms in simplicity. When the Mashiach comes, they will be the ones to place the crown on his head.

Anger and Jealousy

To truly harness the energy of Gevurah, we must also control our anger. Like the process of tzimtzum which is a necessary prelude to any creation (see p. 29), the energy of Gevurah can give rise to new worlds, shaping and actualizing our thoughts. That same energy, used in the wrong way—for example, as an explosion of selfishness or self-aggrandizement—will drive our goal out of reach. An angry person operates with limited vision, losing focus of what he sees. All that he does see is the object of his anger, ignoring extenuating circumstances, other justifications, or even a plea for mercy on the part of the "culprit."

The only way to keep our attention fixed on our goals is to transform anger into compassion (*Likutey Moharan* I, 18:2). When we feel ourselves becoming angry with someone, we should ensure we do nothing unkind, but rather show kindness. This channeling of the energy of Gevurah into Chesed binds us to a higher level beyond our feelings of the moment and lets us reach out to something that is currently beyond our level—i.e., our goal. Through this act we can even grasp a vision of the Ultimate Goal, the World to Come.

> When we overcome our anger, we draw down the spirit of Mashiach, and it is reckoned as if through us the world, and all that is in it, was created. We then merit a good livelihood, we can pray to God without any extraneous motivation, and we can bring from potentiality to actuality all the mitzvot and good deeds that we must fulfill (*Likutey Moharan* I, 66).

The Talmud teaches (*Berakhot* 61b), "The liver is angry."[12] Rebbe Nachman explains that an overexcited person is one whose "liver" has taken control of his emotions and polluted them, causing him to act like a wild beast. On the other hand, a person who controls his anger is at peace with himself. His most human side becomes apparent for all to see (*Likutey Moharan* I, 57:6).

---

[12] The liver is characterized this way because it must constantly toil at filtering and purifying the blood of the poisons which the body absorbs.

Similar to anger, jealousy can surge within a person and thrust him into a state of rage. The main difference between the two is that anger tends to dissipate after a while, but jealousy can persist and burn continuously, eating up a person's very self. Jealousy, like anger, is one of the most harmful characteristics a person can have, and diverts him from his goals.

Reb Noson notes that a good person—one who sees the good in himself and others and always tries to bring out the best in everyone—is represented by a beneficial eye (the attribute of Chesed). A jealous person—one who sees the bad in himself and others and arouses ill feeling, hatred and arguments—is represented by the "evil eye." Notwithstanding his own good fortune, a jealous person will harbor ill will towards anyone who possesses even a fraction of what he has (*Likutey Halakhot, Ha'Oseh Shliach Ligvot Chovo* 3:11).[13]

Yet jealousy, like anger, has a beneficial side. One who is jealous of another's wisdom, for example, and applies himself to attain that which he lacks, uses jealousy in a productive way. Our Sages extol the benefits of *kinas sofrim* (jealousy among scholars) for producing more and greater Torah thoughts (see *Bava Batra* 21a).

We must apply our Gevurah—our ability to set boundaries in life—to learn when and where we can expend our energies in the most beneficial way, to establish the road to success, and to focus on and attain our goals.

---

[13] In one of his teachings, the ARI cites the "*Shin-Ayin* Lights" (370 Lights of the Face) that represent the Light of Keter as it devolves. Opposing these Lights is the *ASh* (worm, spelled *Ayin-Shin*), which consumes whatever it sees. These concepts parallel the benevolence of the good eye and the envy of the evil eye. The Talmud thus teaches (*Shabbat* 152b), "He who is jealous, his bones decay," for the "worm" of jealousy eats away at him (cf. *Shaar Hagilgulim* #23).

8

⚜

TIFERET
The Light of Truth and Peace

Tiferet translates as beauty and represents the harmony and truth that can, and do, illuminate our lives. The Hebrew word *tiPhERet* shares the same root as the words *Pe'ER* (beauty) and *PuRah* (branches). In the array of the Sefirot we find Tiferet in the center column, branching out to the right and left sides, receiving from the upper Sefirot and transferring their bounty to the lower levels. This, in a sense, is the true beauty of Tiferet, which is able to unite and harmonize different energies and channel them in a manner that brings beneficence to all.

As a symbol of truth and unity, Tiferet also represents peace. We see this on a human scale when families or groups manage to live at peace with each other despite their differences. It is also evident on a Divine scale as God, Who is One, is at the same time the Ultimate Truth, the Ultimate Unity and the Ultimate Giver of Peace. Thus Tiferet manifests the peace that results from unity despite divergent approaches.[14]

---

[14] Tiferet is sometimes called *Rachamim* (Mercy) and sometimes *Mishpat* (fair and proper Judgment). Tiferet is therefore Merciful Judgment—judgment tempered with mercy. The function of a judge in a dispute is to adjudicate between contending parties and help them arrive at a peaceful settlement. Although we as individuals

Tiferet also corresponds to Torah study. Like Tiferet, the Torah has many "branches." Starting with a single verse or phrase from Scripture, the commentators cull references from other parts of Torah to develop and reveal different shades of meaning and even new ideas in the original verse. Those familiar with the study of Torah—both its Written and Oral components, including the Kabbalah—are aware of the Torah's ability to guide a person from the first thought (i.e., teaching) towards a logical conclusion of the subject matter. What better way to learn how to grasp our own potential than by applying the analytical reasoning of God's Law to practical use?

Naturally, everyone claims to have the truth and, interestingly enough, every person does, in one way or another. We all have our own individual element or perspective of what truth is. As for the real core of truth—well, that's a different story. Rebbe Nachman's teachings on the subjects of truth, harmony and peace are concrete pillars that will help us master these attributes.

Once Reb Noson's family put pressure on him to accept a job offer as a rabbi in a certain town. Reb Noson was reluctant to take the position because it might interfere with his learning sessions with Rebbe Nachman. When he discussed the pros and cons with the Rebbe, the latter asked him, "Who else should be the rabbi? One who doesn't know the answers?"

Reb Noson was taken aback. "Rebbe! Is that the truth? Should I take the job?"

Rebbe Nachman replied, "Yes. That's the truth?"

Hearing the inflection in the Rebbe's voice, Reb Noson persisted, "But Rebbe, is that the *emeser emes* (the real truth)?"

Rebbe Nachman then answered, "No! The real truth is for you not to accept that position." (In this case, it would have hindered Reb Noson's spiritual growth.)

---

may perceive truth in different ways, a truly wise judge can help us to recognize, accept and even bridge the vast differences between us so that we can live in harmony. This is the manifestation of Tiferet.

Truth exists for everyone. But there is a core to the truth, and this is what we must seek out.

Rebbe Nachman addresses these variations in truth. "If my perspective is right, why listen to another? But can I be wrong? If so, what is the real truth? If truth is one, and I have at least an element of truth, then why am I confused? Why can't I find a simple solution? Why does darkness surround me?" The Rebbe answers:

> No matter what, you can encourage and fortify yourself with the truth, since truth is the light of God Himself and no darkness can obscure it. There is no impurity or aspect of evil in the world that does not contain an opening through which you can escape— it is just that you do not see it because of the great darkness that prevails there. But through the truth, God Himself radiates light for you, and even in the depths you can see and will be able to find an opening of hope through which you can go out from darkness to light and truly draw close to God at all times (*Likutey Moharan* I, 112).

Thus, truth exists within everyone, but there are always obstructions. Let's take prayer as an example. As soon as we stand up to pray, we are often bombarded by extraneous thoughts and fantasies that take our minds far from where we want them to be. At such a time, Rebbe Nachman recommends, "The best remedy is to make sure that the words emerge from your lips in truth. Every word that comes from your mouth in truth and sincerity will provide you with an exit from the darkness which is trapping you, and then you will be able to pray properly. This is a fundamental principle whenever you are praying or meditating. You may feel unable to say a single word because of the intense darkness and confusion that hedge you in on all sides. But make sure that whatever you do say, you say as honestly and as truthfully as you possibly can.

"For example, you could at least say truthfully the words, 'God, send help.' You may not be able to put much enthusiasm into the words, but you can still make yourself say them sincerely and mean what you say quite literally. The truth of your words will send you light and you will be able to pray, with the help of God" *(Likutey Moharan I, 9:4)*.

Prayer is a "one-on-one" situation. There's God and there's you. God is right there, but how do you "know" it? How can you feel it? Try truth. Try honesty. Try to say the words as honestly as you can. Reach out to Him. Then you'll feel God reaching out to you. You are honest. God is Truth. They are one and the same. You are one and the same, merging with God, tapping into His Limitless Resources, His Limitless Potential.

And always know: "When you speak truthfully, you are blessed with Heaven's lovingkindness" *(Aleph-Bet Book, Salvation and Miracles, A27)*. When you allow truth to permeate your inner being, you open up the flow of Chesed (Lovingkindness) from Above and create channels to receive that bounty and prepare for its transference to other people too. This ties in with another teaching: "Truth will bring the final redemption" *(Aleph-Bet Book, Truth, B9)*. When man faces up to his responsibilities and is willing to accept the real truth, his potential can be realized.

Rebbe Nachman adds, "The only way to come to truth is by drawing close to the true Tzaddikim and by following their advice without deviating from their words to the right or to the left" *(Likutey Moharan I, 7:3)*. Tzaddikim are individuals who have already attained truth and know the importance of communicating that truth. We must be discerning, however: There are great people, Tzaddikim in their own right, who nevertheless have not attained absolute truth. As the Rebbe explains:

> Know! A true teaching from the mouth of the true Tzaddik, even in worldly matters, is more precious than the Torah teachings of another Tzaddik. This is because it is possible that in the Torah teachings of the other Tzaddik lies a great admixture. But the teachings that the true Tzaddik utters are nothing but truth. And because they are only truth, without any admixture, there is nothing more precious *(Likutey Moharan I, 192:1)*.

Rebbe Nachman is telling us that there are many levels and perspectives of truth. Even good and righteous people might not

THE ENERGIES OF THE SEFIROT

have attained absolute truth. Therefore, we must keep searching, no matter what we think we've accomplished. This also applies to developing our potential, because we may think we've gone as far as we can without realizing that everyone has resources that haven't been tapped yet. Through honest searching, we can learn more about ourselves and our abilities than we ever thought possible.

Torah Study

Torah study is a vital tool in our pursuit. It enhances our perception of truth.

> Without Torah, it is impossible to live. At times you can burn with a fiery passion for God, but the passion may be excessive and could engulf you completely. Torah study has the power to cool the flames and allow you to survive. There are other times when you can burn with a desire for the temptations of this world. The fire of these passions could burn your entire body. Learning Torah protects you from this. The fire within you becomes extinguished and you can live. Torah is the source of all true life (*Likutey Moharan* I, 78).

The Torah is a great Chesed of God: He gave us this guide to navigate through the vicissitudes of life. Additionally, the Torah's laws act as boundaries and parameters for life, so that Torah also parallels Gevurah. Its teachings come together in Tiferet (perfection, truth and harmony), as in (*Psalms* 19:8), "The Torah of God is perfect." For these reasons, Rebbe Nachman placed great emphasis on Torah study. "Steal time from your business and other activities in order to study Torah," he recommends. "Even if you are burdened with many obligations and duties, you cannot be so pressed that you cannot snatch some period each day to devote to Torah" (*Likutey Moharan* I, 284).

> Attempt to go through all our sacred books in the course of your lifetime. You will then have visited every place in the Torah. The very rich constantly travel from land to land. They spend huge amounts just so that they should be able to say that they have been to some faraway place. You should likewise travel everywhere in

the Torah. In the Future Life, you will be able to say that you have visited every place in our sacred literature. At that time, you will also remember everything you have ever learned (*Rabbi Nachman's Wisdom* #28).

Torah study should not be regarded as an unpleasant duty. One has to know *how* to look into it, and seek guides to navigate its byways. Rebbe Nachman suggests two additional approaches that can ease the transition and help one "taste" the sweetness of Torah. The first is to break your pride completely. Never take credit for yourself; give all the credit to God alone. The second is to give charity, especially to charitable causes in the Land of Israel. This is the way to draw from the "mentality" of the Land of Israel and thereby taste the sweetness of Torah wisdom (*Likutey Moharan* II, 71).

The importance of Torah study cannot be overstated. Rebbe Nachman says that all our prayers and requests are accepted in the merit of our learning. Moreover, Torah students are endowed with a special grace that makes others agree to fulfill their needs, whether material or spiritual (*Likutey Moharan* I, 1:1).

Remember, however, that "a person cannot merit Torah except through humility" (*Likutey Moharan* I, 14:4). When we attain any goal for which we've worked hard, it's natural to feel pride in ourselves and our achievements. We must not let those feelings spill over into negating others. Humility, which is a prerequisite for the study of Torah, also goes hand in hand with Tiferet. Here are some tips for achieving inner peace and harmony with others:

Always be at peace with yourself. It is no good if the different aspects of your personality are in conflict with one another. Also aim for harmony in your relationships with the outside world. Regardless of whether things appear to be good or bad, always look for God in whatever happens to you. Do not allow yourself to be thrown off course by anything. Have faith that everything you experience day by day is a favor and a blessing. This applies even to your hardships and suffering. Believe and know that everything is for your ultimate good. Its sole purpose is to draw you closer to God, if you truly desire it.

The same basic principle applies in your relationship with friends. Love them and be at peace with them regardless of their behavior, even if they make things difficult for you. Always judge them on the scale of merit and find good in them. Interpret everything in a good light and remind yourself that your friends' intentions were not as bad as you imagined. It is very important to strive for relations of love and peace with your friends and with all Israel. The way to achieve this is through the Torah, which is called "peace," and through the Tzaddikim, who are also called "peace" (*Likutey Moharan* I, 33:1).

When peace exists between people, they speak with one another and consider together the ultimate purpose of this world and its vanities. They explain the truth to one another—that in the end nothing will remain of a person except what he prepared for himself for the World to Come. For, "Neither silver, nor gold, nor precious stones nor pearls accompany a person at his death; only his Torah study and good deeds" (*Avot* 6:9). As a result of this honest dialogue, we can cast aside our false worship of money and draw ourselves closer to the truth, turning towards God, His Torah and spiritual work (*Likutey Moharan* I, 27:1-2).

Pursuing peace brings to trust in God.

Truth promotes peace (*Aleph-Bet Book, Peace and Tranquility*, A5-6).

9

NETZACH, HOD
The Light of Attachment

As the energy of the upper Sefirot is channeled into ever more diminishing and specific proportions to the lower Sefirot, we begin to see a more exacting and refined view of our goals.

This process can be easily visualized in the human anatomy that parallels the Sefirot. Chesed, Gevurah and Tiferet manifest in the upper part of the body, in the arms and torso that represent upward, downward and outward movement, symbolizing the "larger" viewpoint and sweep of all we may accomplish. Still, the ideas are too broad, the goal yet imprecise. Our energies must be further distilled through Netzach and Hod. These Sefirot parallel the legs, which, though they can move in several directions, have limited mobility compared to the arms.

The legs are the main pillars that support the body, as well as the principal means of human locomotion. Spiritually, the legs represent the lower and outer reaches of man. With his legs, man makes contact with the physical ground. When he pushes his legs against the earth, he is able to lift himself and rise above it. With the energies of Netzach and Hod (which correspond to the right and left legs, respectively) we can learn to be firmly grounded even while we are striving for great heights. At the same time, we won't lose sight of our limitations despite our yearning for things beyond.

The Hebrew word *NetZaCH* shares the same root as *l'NatZei'aCH* (to gain dominance, victory, eternal). As the Sefirah that follows Tiferet (truth), Netzach represents the necessity of being honest in victory, as in (*I Samuel* 15:29), *"Netzach Yisrael lo yeshaker*—The Eternal [and Victorious One] of Israel will not lie." Attainment of Netzach also means that others recognize the value of our achievements and our opponents call for a total cessation of hostilities. Even if there is no direct opposition to our objectives, there may still be "talk" and perhaps ridicule. But Netzach—true victory—brings about the cessation of even this antagonism.

HOD means splendor. It is related to the word *HODa'ah* (admission), connoting a state of submission and empathy. The "splendor" of Hod is manifest in how one honors the Torah and Torah scholars.[15] Hod reflects the "admission" that Torah is the means by which we come to learn about God; by submission to a Higher Power, we can formulate and better direct ourselves towards our goals. Hod also mirrors empathy, as we direct our energies to support the weak—including those who are physically weak, financially insecure, and emotionally or spiritually vulnerable.

These Sefirot direct us to avoid "walking in the path of the wicked" (cf. *Psalms* 1:1). The Hebrew word for foot, *ReGeL*, is etymologically related to *leRaGeiL* (to slander). By acquiring the attributes of Netzach and Hod, we minimize our involvement with slander and evil speech (see *Likutey Moharan* I, 14:12). Our efforts will lead to peace among people, furthering the influence of Tiferet (peace). Peace—the absence of conflict in our minds and surroundings—is naturally the best state in which to concentrate and focus on our objectives.

---

[15] Since Netzach and Hod border on Tiferet, their adjacent position reflects their support of Torah (which corresponds to Tiferet, as explained in the previous chapter).

Netzach is an extension of Chesed, while Hod is an extension of Gevurah. Both Netzach and Hod are necessary in order to achieve a balance in life, as we must learn not only how to give or to hold back, but also how to receive and acquiesce to others. Using both "legs," we can move forward, confident of success in our efforts, while harboring a healthy awareness that at times we should hold back and submit to forces stronger than ourselves.

This means, on the one hand, that if you are worthy of ascending to a certain level, you must not allow yourself to remain at your current level. No matter where you stand, never be content with your present level. You are always capable of doing and accomplishing more, and are therefore obligated to develop and use that capability. This is Netzach.

On the other hand, if you should fall, regardless of how far and to what extent—even to the very depths of depravity, God forbid—you must never give up hope. Whatever happens, search out and entreat God to help you. You must "take a stand"—that is, remain strong in whichever way you can and whatever position you find yourself. Always choose to retain the vitality of the moment despite the restraints, challenges and opposition that you encounter. This is Hod.

These Sefirot also represent the ability for renewal, to begin again and—despite the challenges that deflect us—to give our goals another chance to be actualized.

Legs have tremendous strength. Practice standing firmly on the ground. When you decide to move forward, do so with conviction. When you must stop and give way, do so without hesitation or regret.

Walking in this manner reveals the secret of self-effacement. The right leg corresponds to self-assertion, the left leg to self-effacement. Walking requires a combination of the two. When you assert yourself, don't push God out of the picture. And when you must efface yourself, don't be fooled into thinking that you are any less of a person. The greatest Tzaddikim knew the secret of self-effacement, and therein lay their greatness. They were able to hold on no matter what challenges they faced, relying on their trust in God and their faith in themselves.

Additionally, Netzach means asserting yourself and understanding your own significance in your search for God. Hod means appreciating your own insignificance. Yet it is that very recognition of your own insignificance vis-à-vis God that allows you to recognize that God is everywhere.

Kabbalistically, Netzach and Hod correspond to the kidneys, whose function is to "advise" a person (*Berakhot* 61a). Just as the kidneys act as a filtering system for the body, retaining necessary fluids and expelling waste matter, one who seeks advice must weigh what he hears, retain the ideas that will help him complete his task, and reject the superfluous. Netzach and Hod direct us to filter the advice necessary to complete our mission.

The Kabbalah almost always speaks of Netzach and Hod as being bound to one another. Similar to fraternal twins, they represent a unique type of attachment, a unity of opposites that still allows for individual growth. The energies of Netzach and Hod allow us to stand on solid ground throughout our lives and develop our latent potential into actual deed.

Rebbe Nachman draws a connection between these two Sefirot and the power of *halikhah* (walking or going). When a person wishes to draw close to God, the Rebbe explains, he must employ the skills of "running" and "returning" (cf. *Ezekiel* 1:14):

> If you progress and reach a particular level of spirituality—be it high or not so high—you should not stop there and be content with your achievement. In this case, the skill you need is to know and believe that you must advance still further. This is the skill of "running." On the other hand, even if you fall to a lower level—even into the lowest pit of Hell, God forbid—you must still not despair in any way. Remain firm and search for God, pleading with Him and begging Him to help in whatever way He can. Even in the lowest pit of Hell, God is present, and even from there it is possible to

be attached to Him. As King David said *(Psalms* 139:8): "If I make Hell my bed, behold, there You are." The skill you need now is "returning" *(Likutey Moharan* I, 6:4).

The word *HaLaKhaH*, from the same root as *HaLiKhaH*, refers to Jewish Law. This suggests that the path we choose should be the lawful one, not the unlawful one. And, just as Netzach and Hod are adjacent energies to Tiferet (Torah, i.e., Law), the skills necessary to develop our forward motion depend on our knowledge of Halakhah.

Barrier Up Ahead

The Kabbalists describe the pathway to God as one of levels rather than a smooth, uphill climb. This model explains why a person who has overcome certain challenges or obstacles may re-encounter them at a later stage in his spiritual journey. He must not think that he has slipped in his efforts and reverted back to the way he "used to be." Rather, at each new level, physical desires, illusions, negative thoughts, confusion and barriers all rise up against him anew. He has not regressed at all; these forces are simply the "welcoming committee" to the next level, where he must do battle with them again. By strengthening himself with determination and refusing to get discouraged, he can overcome them again and continue to rise ever higher *(Likutey Moharan* I, 25:1-3).

Trying to serve God in the face of overwhelming opposition or difficulties can be frustrating. After all, you're trying to serve God and trying to reach your goal. Why should you have to confront challenges when you're doing the right thing? Why aren't the people who *aren't* pursuing the right goals being disturbed? Rebbe Nachman reveals a fascinating insight into the true nature of barriers and obstacles:

> The greater the value of the goal for which you yearn, the bigger the obstacles and barriers that are sent in order to strengthen your desire. For desire is in proportion to the magnitude of the

barriers.... There are always difficulties and obstacles when you try to do anything holy.... You need fierce determination; you must strengthen your desire and willpower in proportion to the greatness of the goal you are aiming for. Then you will succeed in breaking the barriers and attaining your goal. There is no barrier in the world that a person cannot break, so long as he has the desire and willpower to do so (*Likutey Moharan* I, 66:4).

"You may imagine that the barriers you experience in your efforts to serve God are so great that you will never be able to break them," the Rebbe adds. "But this is not true. No one is ever confronted with barriers he cannot break if he really wants to. God only sends obstacles that are within your capacity to overcome if you are determined enough. If you think about it carefully, you will realize that these obstacles are in fact a veil for God Himself. In reality, there are no obstacles at all. They are simply an illusion" (*Likutey Moharan* II, 46).

This insight comes as great encouragement to anyone who has ever decided to improve his situation. Even after a whole lifetime of materialistic pursuits, a person can return to God, and he will surely find Him in the barriers that confront him. These barriers are not meant to be turn-offs from the spiritual path; rather, they are a signal that one is on the right path and should keep moving forward (*Likutey Moharan* I, 115).

The whole reason a person is distanced from God is so that he should rouse himself and ultimately draw even closer. If you fall, the thing to do is to start serving God anew as if you had never even started. This is a cardinal rule in the service of God—to start anew literally every day (*Likutey Moharan* I, 261).

When seeking a goal—any goal—it's important to never lose focus. If we get sidetracked, we need to strengthen ourselves again and again. Despite having made wrong choices, despite the lack of real knowledge of what we should be doing, and even despite intentional errors or sins, we must begin anew. This way, we remain focused. This way, we can still "create" and develop our ideas until they eventually emerge into actuality.

Never let yourself fall completely. There are many ways you can fall. At times your prayer and devotion may seem utterly without meaning. Strengthen yourself and begin anew. Act as if you were just beginning to serve God. No matter how many times you fall, rise up and start again. Do this again and again, for otherwise you will never come close to God. Draw yourself towards God with all your might.

Remain strong, no matter how low you fall. Whether you go up or down, always yearn to come close to God. You may even be brought low, but cry out to God and do everything you can to serve Him in joy. For without this inner strength, you will never be able to truly approach God. Keep pushing until you can do nothing else but serve God all your life. Be ready to do so even without a promise of reward.

You may imagine that you are so far from God that you have no Future Reward. You must still serve Him as you can, even without such promise. It may seem that you are damned, but your responsibility is still there. Continue serving God as best you can. Snatch a good deed, a lesson, a prayer, and God will do what is good in His eyes (*Rabbi Nachman's Wisdom* #48).

Recall that Netzach translates as victory as well as eternal. Reb Noson writes that these meanings are very much interconnected. The only victory that has any real value is an eternal victory (*Likutey Halakhot, Birkhot Pratiyot* 5:2). Reb Noson refers to the pyrrhic victories of kings and conquerors who, in later years, lost wars and kingdoms. Of what value are short-lived triumphs? In our daily lives, this manifests in family quarrels, communal disputes, political divisiveness, etc. Most victories are short-lived, while others come along and wipe out any gains that were ever made. Netzach teaches us to focus on long-lasting, eternal goals. It also means pursuing those goals with boldness.

Hod, on the other hand, teaches us to step back occasionally. As much as we want to take a bold step forward, we must restrain ourselves at times. Here is a good way to look at Hod and understand its great value:

Always feel content with what you have. Take no more from the world than is absolutely essential. Do not live in luxury like so many people do today. People who lack this sense of contentment are referred to in the saying (*Proverbs* 13:25), "The belly of the wicked shall want," because they are always in need of something. Be content with what God has given you, and even out of this minimum, still contribute a portion to charity. This brings about great unification in the worlds above, and blesses the world with abundance (*Likutey Moharan* I, 54:3).

Rebbe Nachman does not glorify poverty. In fact, according to the Kabbalists, Hod indicates wealth. What Rebbe Nachman does advocate is holding back from lusting after the short-term goals of wealth and fame. There's nothing wrong with wealth, as long as it isn't your goal. Conversely, by living simply, you can experience a life of contentment with whatever you have. This gives you the luxury of pursuing the goals you truly seek.

A New Day – A New Start

The secret of a long life, Rebbe Nachman teaches, is to make your days "long" with added holiness. Everyone can fill and enrich each moment of each day with a mitzvah, time spent in Torah study, a thought of God, or a step towards a spiritual goal.

When you start each day, at first it seems very short. The spiritual accomplishments you need to achieve this day weigh heavily upon you. It takes great determination not to be discouraged as you feel the weight of the devotions you have to undertake this day. But be courageous and don't lose heart. Make a start—even if at first things seem heavy and strained and difficult. If you are determined enough, they will become easier and you will find that you can accomplish what you must. With every hour that passes, see to it that you enrich that hour and lengthen it with extra holiness. Do the same with every new day of your life. Let each day be filled with more holiness than the day before. Then you will be blessed with length of days. The root of this skill in living lies in cultivating true fear of Heaven (*Likutey Moharan* I, 60:2-3).

By lengthening your days with holiness, you gain the luxury of a sense of fulfillment: "Today I accomplished!" "Today I achieved!" Keeping focused on your goal yields a great feeling of success.

"The key to everything is the way you start," Rebbe Nachman notes. "All beginnings are difficult because you are trying to turn things from one direction to the opposite direction. But once a start has been made, you begin to get used to the direction you are going in and things are no longer so hard.... Every day you should go 'backwards,' in the sense that you should always try to draw inspiration from the start, which was the hardest thing of all" (*Likutey Moharan* I, 62:5).

Viewing each day as a new start can also help combat other obstacles, such as opposition from family and friends. When we begin the day as if nothing came before—no pressures, no outside influences—we move ourselves closer to the goals we seek. In this way we emulate the fortitude of Abraham, the father of the Jewish People, who focused on his goal of serving God as if he were the only person in the world, paying no attention to his detractors (*Likutey Moharan* II, Foreword).

We mentioned that Netzach and Hod represent the kidneys, the "advisory" organs. In Hebrew, the kidneys are called *klayot* and *betuchot* (*Psalms* 51:8). The word *BeTuChot* shares the same root as *BiTaChon* (trust). We must trust our instincts and have faith in ourselves. We must also trust in God that He will always be with us.

> When you trust in God and look to Him alone for all your needs, a vessel is formed with which you can receive His blessing. What you need will be sent to you, as and when you require it (*Likutey Moharan* I, 76).

These needs include our elusive but much sought-after potential. By developing trust, we create the vessels needed to receive God's blessings. Then we can attain our goals.

ONLY HUMAN

A person must always remember that he is human. We all make mistakes, and may even succumb to temptation and sin outright. Yet through repentance, we can dust ourselves off and start over again. Rebbe Nachman's famous parable, "The Tainted Grain," illustrates this point:

> A king once told his prime minister, who was also his good friend, "I see in the stars that whoever eats any grain that grows this year will go mad. What is your advice?"
>
> The prime minister replied, "We must put aside enough grain so that we will not have to eat from this year's harvest."
>
> The king objected, "But then we will be the only ones who will be sane. Everyone else will be mad. Therefore, they will think that *we* are the mad ones!"
>
> After thinking for a while, the king decided, "It is impossible for us to put aside enough grain for everyone. Therefore, we too must eat this year's grain. But we will make a mark on our foreheads, so that at least we will know that we are mad. I will look at your forehead, and you will look at mine, and when we see this sign, we will know that we are both mad" (*Rabbi Nachman's Stories, Parable #21*).

Every success and failure contributes to the person we are today. By accepting the truth of our situation instead of ignoring or denying it, we can pinpoint our errors, repent for our wrongful deeds, and redirect our energies towards positive accomplishments. We free ourselves to take that bold step forward (to "mark the forehead"), even if that same step is a mark of surrender.

10

YESOD
The Light of Foundation and Righteousness

Yesod translates as foundation and corresponds to the male reproductive organ. Explaining this connection, the Kabbalah refers to Yesod as *Chai Olamim* (Life of the Worlds) (*Zohar* I, 193b). Life—because Yesod serves the very essence and purpose of life, and also because it is said to be "alive" (that is, instrumental in bringing forth life). Worlds—because Yesod sparks the interaction between the Upper Worlds and this world (which is represented by Malkhut, the Sefirah below it). Like the sexual act that gathers and channels all the male's energies into union with the female, Yesod pools the energies of all the preceding Sefirot and channels them into Malkhut, culminating in the realization of our desires, efforts, struggles and successes.

Kabbalistically, the energies which Yesod collects and transfers are called Light. God interacts with the world, and the world with Him, through the agencies of *Or Yashar* (Direct Light) and *Or Chozer* (Reflected Light). As the ARI explains, God sends us His direct bounty to sustain us and allow us to live and perform good deeds. Reciprocally, our good deeds bring God a certain pleasure. Like a loving parent, God rejoices when His children "grow up" and become capable of emulating Him. This is the *nachat* (pleasure) He receives from all the mitzvot that we do. When we strive to emulate God, it is considered as if we are giving something back to Him.

Yesod is the relay station for these two types of Light. In one direction, this Sefirah gathers the energy and bounty from the Sefirot above it and transfers them to Malkhut, from where they are channeled to this world. In the other direction, it receives from Malkhut the offerings of God's creations and sends them back Above. (Malkhut is therefore said to be the "mate" of Yesod.)

Yesod represents one of the greatest human pleasures that exists, touching the deepest levels of the psyche. Pleasure can be either good or evil, as it can lead one in either direction.[16] Our personal level of Yesod can indeed be one of holiness and propel us to search for ever greater levels of Godliness, or it can be redirected into mindless sexual pursuits that lead us away from spirituality.

The Zohar teaches that the person who is very moral deserves the accolade of Tzaddik *(Zohar I, 59b)*. Yesod is also connected to the Tzaddik in the verse *(Proverbs 10:25)*, "The Tzaddik is the *yesod* (foundation) of the world." The Tzaddik represents the highest levels of moral purity, through which he helps to keep the world morally righteous, teach others about God, and bring God's message to mankind. The energy of Yesod elevates him beyond his material desires to the point that he attains his goals and, in so doing, brings joy and pleasure to God.

This Sefirah can help us develop our potential depending on the degree to which we embrace moral values. Like the foundation upon which every building stands, morals are the foundation upon which stand all that we strive to build and accomplish in life. If our morals are upright, our building will stand tall and proud. If our values are corrupt, our life's building will be crooked and marked with blemish.

---

[16] See *Innerspace*, p. 69.

Interestingly, one usually builds a building from the ground up, so Yesod should have been the first Sefirah upon which our subsequent efforts to realize our potential rest. However, Keter (will and purpose) is the first step. Only after a long process do we get to the foundation, to Yesod! (Moreover, our efforts do not reach completion until we access Malkhut.) So what kind of "foundation" is this?

The structure of the Sefirot—both in the traditional ordering and in the three-column arrangement—hints at the answer: Yesod is at the bottom to receive *all* the energies that are transmitted from above. Every energy, starting at the top in Keter, must find its way into Yesod before it can be of benefit to man. So too, every one of our actions reflects the structure of our lives. If we are moral and upright, then our energies will be properly received and directed. If we choose to damage that foundation with amoral thoughts or behaviors, all our energies go to waste, God forbid. If there is no foundation upon which to stand, everything goes to the forces of the Other Side—to our opposition—producing challenges and obstacles that thwart us from creating a fuller and more contented life.

Thus Yesod, a solid foundation, is predicated on living a life as free of sin as possible. If a house has a solid foundation, we are not afraid that it will collapse. By building a strong moral foundation, we keep our lives on solid footing. Yesod implies keeping things together, not living a "loose" life.

In Rebbe Nachman's teachings, the Tzaddik exemplifies the ultimate in morality and Godliness. By describing the Tzaddik's power and accomplishments, Rebbe Nachman shows us how we too can develop our own potential to the maximum levels possible. Let's begin with a glimpse into the Future:

> Every good deed that a person does is made into a lamp. [After death, those who performed good deeds] have lights that burn for a short time, and while they burn, they can use them to explore the King's treasury. But then they burn out, and they can no longer search. Some have many good deeds, which burn longer. These people have more time to probe the celestial treasury. Still others

may have lamps that blaze for an entire day or even longer. But there is one person who possesses the most wonderful lamps of all. These are never extinguished, but burn and shine forever. The owner of these lamps can delve into the King's treasury for as long as he wishes (*Likutey Moharan* I, 275).

After relating this lesson, Rebbe Nachman commented:

From this we can understand that even an ordinary religious person can explore the King's treasury, but only for a given time, as determined by his good deeds. Even this is certainly a most wonderful privilege. You can find wonderful treasures even in this short time and then enjoy them in the Future World forever. All of your Future Life is determined by what you find during that time of exploration. If you are worthy of more time in which the lamps created by your deeds shine, you will certainly find more good in the King's treasury. It all depends on how long your lamps can burn. The light of a great Tzaddik is never extinguished. His exploration of the King's treasury can go on forever (*Rabbi Nachman's Wisdom* #134).

A Tzaddik does not live for himself or his own glory, but to serve God and to draw others close to Him. His "lamps" are filled with Torah study, prayer and good deeds, which he possesses in abundance. He helps others understand that everyone has a purpose in life and there are rewards for our efforts, no matter how infinitesimal they may seem. The Tzaddik always encourages people to establish goals and pursue them, as illustrated in this story:

Rebbe Nachman once told us that in Jerusalem there is a synagogue to which all the dead people on earth are brought. As soon as someone in this world dies, he is brought there at once to be judged as to where his place should be. In this synagogue sits the court that hands down these judgments and allocates each person the place he deserves.

When the dead are brought there, they are brought in clothing.[17] Sometimes a dead person's clothing is missing something. One

---

[17] Both the lamps mentioned above and the garments mentioned here refer to Torah study, prayer and good deeds (*Rabbi Nachman's Wisdom* #23).

person may be missing a sleeve, another a piece from the edge of his garment, and so on. Everything depends on a person's actions in his lifetime [because his clothing after death corresponds to his deeds]. The verdict depends on the clothes he has when he is brought there, and his place is allocated accordingly.

Once, a dead person was brought there completely naked. He had no clothes whatsoever. The verdict was that he should be cast into the hollow sling[18] and destroyed, God forbid, because he was completely naked. However, a certain Tzaddik came with one of his own garments and threw it over the person.

The court asked, "Why are you giving him one of your own garments?" The court took exception to this, because why should the dead man be given a garment and be saved with clothing that was not his? The Tzaddik answered: "I have to send this man on a mission for my own purposes, and for this reason I am entitled to dress him in one of my own garments." This is how the Tzaddik saved the dead man from the bitter penalty of the hollow sling.

The Rebbe told this story to demonstrate the tremendous power of the true Tzaddik to save his followers in the World of Truth (*Tzaddik* #228).

Each person performs some good deed in this world; some perform many. Each has his Future Reward waiting for him, plus the additional treasures he can search for in the King's treasury. But as we have seen, the Tzaddik has "lamps" that burn forever. If the Tzaddik can spare a lamp or a garment for one who is naked and undeserving, he can also share the light of these lamps with those who attach themselves to him. One who comes close to the Tzaddik, learning from him how to do the right things and how to serve God altruistically, reaps rewards well beyond his own efforts.

---

[18] A form of punishment in the Next World known as the *kaf hakela* (slingshot), because the soul is tossed and thrown about for a long period until it can be redeemed.

THE TURKEY PRINCE

Not only can the Tzaddik help a person ready himself for the World to Come, he is always available to work with a person in this world, guiding and encouraging him to develop his potential. Rebbe Nachman illustrates this relationship in his famous parable, "The Turkey Prince":

A royal prince once became mad and thought that he was a turkey. He felt compelled to sit naked under the table, pecking at bones and pieces of bread like a turkey. The royal physicians all gave up hope of ever curing him of this madness, and the king suffered tremendous grief.

A sage then came and said, "I will undertake to cure him."

The sage undressed and sat naked under the table next to the prince, picking crumbs and bones. "Who are you?" asked the prince. "What are you doing here?"

"And you?" replied the sage. "What are you doing here?"

"I am a turkey," said the prince.

"I am also a turkey," said the sage.

They sat together like this for some time, until they became good friends. One day, the sage signaled the king's servants to throw him shirts. He said to the prince, "What makes you think that a turkey can't wear a shirt? You can wear a shirt and still be a turkey." With that, the two of them put on shirts.

After a while, he signaled again, and they threw him pants. Just as before, he said, "What makes you think that you can't be a turkey if you wear pants?"

The sage continued in this manner until they were both completely dressed. Then he signaled again, and they were given regular food from the table. Again the sage said, "What makes you think that you will stop being a turkey if you eat good food? You can eat whatever you want and still be a turkey." They both ate the food.

Finally, the sage said, "What makes you think a turkey must sit under the table? Even a turkey can sit at the table."

The sage continued in this manner until the prince was completely cured (*Rabbi Nachman's Stories, Parable #25*).

So it is with us. We are great human beings—princes and princesses who have enormous potential—but we often opt for the easy way out and act like turkeys. Yet the Tzaddikim, who know our potential, do not despair of us. Though they live on a very lofty plane, they are willing to descend to our level and be with us, sharing their ideas and successes and implanting their teachings in our hearts. By following their advice, we will reclaim our original prominence and royalty.

Moral Living

Rebbe Nachman teaches that everyone can become a Tzaddik, even if he or she is not a scholar. One requires scholarship to achieve deep perceptions of Godliness, but even a simple person can attain the level of a righteous Jew (*Rabbi Nachman's Wisdom #76*). This is because the level of Tzaddik (Yesod) is dependent on *living* a moral life, not on what (or who) one knows.

Rebbe Nachman's definition of morality encompasses moral living in all areas, including financial dealings and sexual relations. The Rebbe speaks about guarding one's thoughts against lustful thinking and guarding one's tongue against improper speech (see *Likutey Moharan* I, 29). The name given to all these activities is *shmirat habrit* (guarding the covenant). This covenant refers to the *brit milah* (the covenant of circumcision) which was enacted between God and Abraham and, by extension, between God and all of Abraham's descendants (see *Genesis* 17). In the Kabbalah and Rebbe Nachman's writings, this covenant refers mainly to sexual purity.

Guarding the covenant means keeping one's brit (i.e., the male reproductive organ) clean from sin. One should marry and procreate, but abstain from extramarital relationships and homosexuality.

Other blemishes include marriages proscribed by Torah law and relationships outside of marriage. A common error is that there is nothing wrong with masturbation. Although this act is not listed as one of the 365 Torah prohibitions, it is viewed as the most severe of all violations of the covenant (*Even Ha'ezer* 23:1). (But see below for a discussion of how one can rectify all these transgressions.)

Rebbe Nachman offers several tools to attain morality and a guarded covenant. He teaches:

> Morality and humility are interconnected. True honor belongs to the person who has a guarded covenant. One cannot be pure if he is arrogant. One cannot be humble if he defiles his brit (*Likutey Moharan* I, 11:2-3). On the other hand, immorality brings shame and disgrace upon a person (*Likutey Moharan* I, 38:5).

We have seen that Keter, the first of the Sefirot, represents humility and humbleness. If a person's first impulse (will, i.e., Keter) is for good thoughts, good deeds and positive results, then the energy which ultimately emerges in Yesod will yield beneficial results. If a person is arrogant, the energy that descends becomes corrupted. The opposite also holds true. If one's primal instincts are laced with positive thinking, but he later uses that energy to blemish his brit, his immorality will corrupt his humility. He will become arrogant, leading to degradation and disgrace. Thus, the first tool for a guarded covenant and moral living is humility.

A second tool is unadulterated speech. "Morality and a clean tongue are dependent on each other" (*Likutey Moharan* I, 19:3). A clean tongue means speaking words of encouragement (Chesed), offering constructive rebuke (Gevurah), telling the truth (Tiferet) and extending magnanimous and empathetic feelings to others (Netzach and Hod). A clean tongue also avoids gossip, slander, falsehood, flattery and idle talk. The advantages of clean speech are seen in the Reflected Light that Malkhut (which represents the mouth) returns Above, for clean speech will generate enormous energy to return that which it was given.

A third tool is staying focused on what we have, not on what we want. The former helps us maintain morality; the latter steers us off course. Rebbe Nachman explains: "Avarice and immorality are interconnected. Defiling the brit causes a person to descend into the quicksand of avarice, where he can't see his way beyond material pursuit" (*Likutey Moharan* I, 23:2-3). One who constantly seeks more physical satisfaction can never have enough material wealth either. Of course, we all want a good life. But we must learn to be happy and rejoice with what we have already achieved in order to remain focused on that which we desire.[19] Allowing immoral thoughts and deeds to take charge of our lives enslaves us to our cravings.

To attain morality, we also require prayer. Conversely, we cannot attain true, directed prayer except through a guarded covenant. The way to solve this dilemma is by executing justice (*Likutey Moharan* I, 2:2-4). Executing justice refers to Mishpat, as defined above (see p. 116, footnote 14). True justice is attained when one harnesses opposing energies and unites them harmoniously; this also represents a moral decision to do the right thing. We see justice in action when we balance the opposing energies of Chesed (right side) and Gevurah (left side) in the center column, Tiferet. The energy of Tiferet then descends through Netzach and Hod, harmonizing again in the center column in Yesod. Making just decisions ensures moral living, energizing the covenant with bounty to deliver to Malkhut.

True moral living doesn't happen overnight. We must combat many temptations and challenges to control our behavior and conversations, let alone the thoughts and sights that force us to keep "holding the reins." But the more we work on ourselves, the more we bolster our morality, and eventually we can attain a purer view of life and its meaning.

Rebbe Nachman compares a person to a pot of water that seems perfectly clear. When the pot is placed on a fire and begins to boil, however, all the impurities in the water rise to the surface and must be skimmed away. The original "clear water" is merely an illusion

---

[19] This is why Netzach and Hod are the channels through which the energies of the Sefirot reach Yesod, as explained in the previous chapter.

that is exposed by the "heat" of challenges and frustrations. In the same way, before a person embarks on his quest for positive goals, good and evil are completely mixed together within him. The impurities are so closely united with the good that they are unrecognizable. But when he makes the effort to improve and draw close to the true Tzaddikim, he lights the fires of purification that bring his errant behavior and wrongful approaches to the surface. Then he can remove the dirt and impurities, and become truly pure and clear (*Rabbi Nachman's Wisdom* #79).

The rewards of morality are many. Rebbe Nachman enumerates:

Morality brings compassion, faith and livelihood (*Likutey Moharan* I, 31:9).

Morality brings peace (ibid., 27).

One who attains morality can "see" God, as in (*Job* 19:26), "From my flesh I behold God" (*Likutey Moharan* I, 22:5).

Morality gives a person the ability to draw God's blessing in a bountiful manner (ibid., 36).

The greater the degree of morality, the more its beneficence extends to one's children (ibid., 39).

THE TREASURE

Every person can attain great degrees of morality, if he so desires. Each person has precious treasures buried deep within his psyche; he just needs help to mine them. This is where his yearnings can merge with the Tzaddik's greatness to bring forth his potential. Rebbe Nachman illustrates this idea with a parable:

A man once dreamed that there was a great treasure under a bridge in Vienna. He traveled to Vienna and stood near the bridge, trying to figure out what to do. He did not dare search for the treasure by day, because of the many people who were there.

An officer passed by and asked, "What are you doing, standing here and thinking?" The man decided that it would be best to tell the whole story and ask for help, hoping that the officer would share the treasure with him. He told the officer about his dream.

"A Jew is concerned only with dreams!" the officer exclaimed. "I also had a dream, and I also saw a treasure. It was in a small house, under the cellar."

In relating his dream, the officer accurately described the man's city and house. The man rushed home, dug under his cellar and found the treasure. He said, "Now I know that I had the treasure all along. But in order to find it, I had to travel to Vienna!" (*Rabbi Nachman's Stories, Parable #24*).

The same thing happens to us when we want to realize our goals, Rebbe Nachman says. Each person has the "treasure"—the potential to go very far and to attain great levels. But in order to realize it, he must travel to the Tzaddik. Because the Tzaddik lives a moral and fulfilled life, he is able to guide each person to develop his own treasures.

Tikkun HaKlali

The benefits of morality are obvious. Yet it is all too easy to blemish the covenant and bring about a host of negative consequences. These include:

A defiled covenant can defile the air a person breathes and so pollute that air as to negatively affect others around him (*Likutey Moharan* I, 43).

Immorality builds false faiths and trust (ibid., 60:8).

Immorality is akin to theft and stealing (ibid., 69).

Should a person succumb, however, all is not lost. In a highly original and beneficial teaching, Rebbe Nachman reveals the existence of a spiritual cure-all that can actually atone for the worst sins while at the same time put the penitent back on the right track. Keying into the Kabbalists' description of Yesod as a *Sefirah Klalit* (a Comprehensive Sefirah, since all the energies from the higher levels must at some point enter into Yesod), Rebbe Nachman revealed a *Tikkun HaKlali* (a Comprehensive or General Remedy) that can help a person escape the quagmire he has created for himself by blemishing his brit *(Likutey Moharan* I, 29).

To explain how the Tikkun HaKlali works, the Rebbe uses the bloodstream of the human body as an example. The heart pumps oxygen-rich blood into the aorta, which branches into the secondary arteries that feed the body's organs and tissues. As they travel further away from the heart, the arteries get smaller and smaller until they turn into capillaries, which deliver oxygen and nutrients directly to each cell and remove carbon dioxide and waste products. Leaving the cells, the capillaries grow larger and larger until they turn into veins, which return oxygen-poor blood to the heart. The entire system depends on the heart—the pumping source that sends the blood to the most remote and minor parts of the body to ensure good health. Any malfunction at the lower levels of the system can usually be traced to a weak or blocked blood flow from the heart.

Similarly, in the spiritual realm, a major or minor transgression can be rectified by going back to the source of the law or mitzvah and invoking the energy to "pump" the rectification necessary out to the extremities of one's behavior. The Tikkun HaKlali goes to the root of the mitzvah and rectifies it at its source. Whatever offshoots the mitzvah has can then be corrected with *teshuvah* (repentance).

Let's consider a few examples. If someone engages in financial irregularities, such as shortchanging customers, he can physically atone for his mistake by reimbursing his clients and spiritually rectify his error by giving charity, which is also a financial act. Charity thus serves as a "general remedy" for any financial errors or wrongful transactions that one may have committed. (Of course, one cannot intentionally make financial "errors" and then rely on giving charity to repair his misdeeds.)

Another example cited by the Rebbe is wrongful speech. Blemished speech hurts many people. How can one retract his words? He can't—but he can invoke a "general remedy" of speech by praising God and the Tzaddikim. Beneficial speech that contains good messages and conveys honest intentions can rectify wrongful speech at its source.

The Tikkun HaKlali is most effective in the area of sexual transgressions, since the offshoots of these sins are many. A lustful thought, a lewd wink, flirting and suggestive body language are but a few of the "minor" repercussions of a blemish of Yesod. How much more devastating are the major sins of illegal cohabitation and wasted seed! In the latter case, according to the Kabbalists, the sparks of holiness that are affected are banished to the realm of the Other Side. Without active rectification, it may take thousands of years to effect repairs to those sparks.

Rebbe Nachman teaches that the rectification process begins in the mind. When a person sets his mind to repair a blemish, he draws energy directly from the source. All sexual blemishes are rooted in the mind, since man's thought process eventually leads to the acts he commits.

The second step is the recital of ten specific psalms, in this order: 16, 32, 41, 42, 59, 77, 90, 105, 137, 150.

Rebbe Nachman explains in several lessons why reciting these Ten Psalms are effective (see *Likutey Moharan* I, 29, 205; *Likutey Moharan* II, 92). It is beyond the scope of this book to elaborate on these reasons, but we can offer this insight: The power of psalms is drawn from the Ten Types of Song, which parallel the Ten Sefirot (see *Tikkuney Zohar* #13, *Pesachim* 117a). Kabbalistically, song parallels the highest of levels, which in our discussion refers to the mind (the Mochin, the upper Sefirot). When we "sing" and praise God, we draw the power of the highest levels down to the lower levels, drawing the energy necessary to rectify our blemishes.[20]

Rebbe Nachman offers additional ways to rectify sexual sins. One is by giving charity. When a person blemishes his brit, he wastes his seed, his bounty. By giving charity, he redirects "wasted" bounty

---

[20] See *Rabbi Nachman's Tikkun*, published by the Breslov Research Institute.

back into worthwhile causes, strengthening the realm of holiness (*Likutey Moharan* I, 264).

Another way to rectify this particular blemish of Yesod is by drawing others close to God. Wasted seed, which represents precious sparks of holiness lost to the Other Side, is called *KeRY* in Hebrew. By drawing those who are distant from God closer to Him, we recover those precious (*YaKaR*) sparks and bring them back to the realm of holiness (*Likutey Moharan* I, 14:end).

Taken together, recital of the Tikkun HaKlali, thoughts of repentance, and the giving of charity can mitigate even the most severe sins and return a person to the path of moral virtue. By unblocking the energies that were obstructed through the blemishing of one's brit, a person can open himself again to receive and transmit the energies of the upper Sefirot in a positive way, putting his goals back on a firm footing.

11

❧

MALKHUT
The Light of Faith and Prayer

Malkhut translates as kingship and implies authority, similar to that of a monarch who wields power over his domain. In a deeper sense, Malkhut represents the Authority of God. As mentioned earlier (see p. 59), Malkhut is the vessel that manifests the Light of Keter. God's Light originates at such a lofty level that we are unable to access it; it must be filtered down through all Ten Sefirot until it reaches Malkhut, from where it can shine onto us and our world.

By mastering all the energies that devolve until they reach Malkhut, we can attain the right to authority. We can become an authority in our field. We can be an authority to others. Through Malkhut, we can learn to exercise control and to use power beneficially for ourselves, our neighbors and communities. Though power often corrupts those who wield it, the fact that we have grounded our efforts on the moral base of Yesod (see previous chapter) helps us act with controlled energy rather than dictatorial whim.

Conceptually, Malkhut represents the mouth. It is the mouth that issues the king's edicts. Furthermore, just as a person reveals his innermost thoughts when he speaks them aloud, Malkhut represents the revelation of God and His Kingdom. When we perform acts that evoke God's Malkhut (such as the recital of the Shma, which the Talmud explains is *"kabbalat ol Malkhut Shamayim*—accepting the yoke of the Kingdom of Heaven"), we draw the energy of Malkhut (control and power) into our lives. As Rebbe Nachman teaches, "Everything we do—praying, Torah study, performing mitzvot, eating, earning a livelihood and much more—has one fundamental aim: to reveal the kingship of God" (*Likutey Moharan* I, 77).

Malkhut is also said to correspond to one's mate. No one can attain his goals on his own. All life is a series of give-and-take relationships that unify benefactor and beneficiary (see p. 53). Just as a husband and wife unite to bring about the birth of their child, so too all the higher energies (the benefactor) unite with Malkhut (the beneficiary) to "give birth" to our ideas and our potential.

We can access this Sefirah and release its energy into our lives with two powerful tools: faith and prayer.

Faith

Faith is a key component of Malkhut. Without faith—including faith in ourselves (see p. 38)—our ability to do and accomplish would never materialize. Faith helps us gain control over our lives and make and carry out decisions with a sense of responsibility. Our faith also builds up our Malkhut, helping us gain control over our objectives and see our goals through to completion.

Faith is one of the most oft-quoted ideas of Rebbe Nachman. Through his teachings we can begin to integrate faith into our lives and develop our "Malkhut potential" to its fullest. Hinting at the structure of the Sefirot through which we have passed, step by step, from Keter through Malkhut, Rebbe Nachman observes: "Through faith you can rise to all levels and attain Desire and Will, which is above everything else" (*Tzaddik* #564).

The Talmud teaches that the prophet Habakkuk included all the commandments of the Torah in one principle (*Habakkuk* 2:4): "The righteous man shall live by his faith." Faith is the foundation and root of all Torah and devotion. Faith must be clear and pure. Faith is the channel for every benefit and blessing (*Rabbi Nachman's Wisdom* #261).

When faith is pure, the blessings received through it are pure. We experience blessing, find contentment and fulfillment, and feel comfortable with ourselves and our achievements. The Rebbe once said, "Pure faith—without any sophistication or proof—is a light that shines by night" (*Rabbi Nachman's Wisdom* #106). Day suggests knowledge (e.g., "clear as day"). Night suggests a lack of knowledge—darkness, confusion and questions that challenge a person who does not have clear vision. Without pure faith, we can get so confused as to mix up the means with the goal. By remaining strong in faith, we will merit a strong and clear light, even in moments of confusion.

Faith is only applicable to something which we do not understand logically. Nevertheless, with perfect faith it becomes revealed to us as if we see it with our own eyes (*Likutey Moharan* I, 62:5).

That is, instead of "seeing is believing," Rebbe Nachman teaches that "believing is seeing"! Faith becomes a person's "eyes," leading him to realize his goals. As long as he remains focused on his objective, even if he does not immediately attain it, he remains "faithful" to his goal. He "sees" his objective clearly, though it's not yet within reach.

It should be mentioned that faith cannot represent a *full* sense of accomplishment. That requires knowledge, while faith is a medium that directs us to knowledge. When we have faith, however, we realize that our achievements have great value and appreciate whatever degree of success we have attained. We know we're "on the way" to greater accomplishments—a reflection of our faith in ourselves.

If you have faith, you are truly alive. When you have faith, every day is filled with good. When things go well, it is certainly good. But when you have troubles, it is also good. For you know that God will eventually have mercy, and the end will be good. Everything must be good, for it all comes from God. The man without faith is not really alive. Troubles befall him and he loses all hope. There is nothing to cheer or comfort him, for he has no faith. He does not feel himself to be under God's Providence and has no good at all. But if you have faith, your life will be good and pleasant (*Rabbi Nachman's Wisdom* #53).

One of the best ways to develop faith is simply to speak about it and continuously declare it. King David says (*Psalms* 89:2), "I will make known Your faith with my mouth." Rebbe Nachman explains that the first step is to affirm our faith verbally, articulating it in various ways. We can always take a moment to say, "I believe in God!" "I believe You created the entire universe!" "I believe You oversee the world and everything in it with Your Divine Providence!" (*Likutey Moharan* II, 44). There are many ways to express faith; the more we do, the more we nurture it. This idea also applies to building faith in oneself. A person who always says to himself, "I believe I can accomplish," will certainly achieve his goals.

In the same lesson about faith, Rebbe Nachman cautions us not to use any words of atheism or mockery when speaking about God (ibid.). The articulation of atheistic words can deflect a person from faith entirely. Like the alcoholic who always has alcohol on his breath, or the chain smoker who exhales the smell of tobacco, a person who speaks atheism will reek of atheism. The opposite is also true: A person who speaks faith, breathes faith.

Faith is actually part of our basic makeup. Reb Noson writes that virtually everything in this world is somehow connected to faith. For example, if there were no faith, no one could conduct business. The storekeeper would always suspect that the customer is out to rob him, and the customer would never be sure he is paying a fair price. If someone wants to do business in another state or country, he must find a representative whom he trusts to buy, sell or trade on his behalf. The global economy would crumble without faith.

Every relationship is also based on faith. Parent and child, husband and wife, friends, neighbors and whole communities must have some basis of trust before they become committed to one another. Once we realize how integral faith is to our lives, we can begin to develop and nurture it (see *Likutey Halakhot, Giluach* 4:2-3).

Honesty is another prerequisite for faith. Kabbalistically speaking, Tiferet (truth and honesty) is the center column that combines the opposing energies of the right and left columns (see p. 116). The same is true of Yesod. All these combined energies filter through to Malkhut. Rebbe Nachman explains that the transfer of truth, honesty and integrity in this manner translates into the need to be honest in our faith without embellishing our perceptions, and to make sure that our beliefs are in areas that are truthful and honest (*Likutey Moharan* I, 7:2-3). It doesn't help our faith at all to place it in false hopes or untruthful goals. On the other hand, being honest about our capabilities and goals can raise our faith to great levels.

Rebbe Nachman places much importance on having faith in the Tzaddikim. We can readily understand this, because Malkhut (faith) is the "mate" of Yesod (the Tzaddik). "We have received the Torah through Moses our teacher and it has been transmitted to us by the awesome Tzaddikim of each generation," Rebbe Nachman describes (see *Avot* 1:1). "There is no question as to their integrity and they can be relied upon without question. All you need to do is follow in their footsteps, believe in God with innocent simplicity, and keep the commandments of the Torah as taught by our holy ancestors" (*Rabbi Nachman's Wisdom* #32).

All faith must be coupled with faith in God, lest we begin to think of ourselves as all-mighty beings who are in control of our own destinies.

> We may think we believe in God as the Ultimate Cause of everything. But in practice, we put our trust in the means. For example, we believe that our livelihood is totally dependent on our business activities and the energy we invest in them—as if without them, God would not have any other means of providing us with our sustenance. In effect, we believe that our business activities are the source of our livelihood and not just the intermediate factor.

Or, we may believe that it is the medicine that produces the cure; as if without it, God would not have any other means of sending healing. Once we believe this, we inevitably become preoccupied with the means—chasing after the right medicaments, throwing ourselves into our work, and so on—and we forget to turn to God, the Source of all things and the Ultimate Cause. It is true that we do have to concern ourselves with the means. But we must not make the mistake of confusing the means with the Ultimate Cause and put our faith in the intermediary. We must have faith in God alone (*Likutey Moharan* I, 62:6).

It is interesting that faith reflects authority, since we have the "authority" to decide how to direct our feelings and emotions towards God and let them become manifest through our faith. Yet what should we do when we feel lost or confused, when our authority cannot seem to exert itself? The Rebbe answers: "You may have many questions and doubts. But when your heart cries out, it shows that you still have the burning spark of faith.... This cry can elevate and strengthen your faith until all difficulties vanish" (*Rabbi Nachman's Wisdom* #146).

If things get really rough, remember this teaching: "If you have doubts about your faith in God, say out loud, 'I believe with perfect faith that God is One—first, last and always'" (*Rabbi Nachman's Wisdom* #142). The more you express your faith, the more you build it, as in (*Psalms* 89:2), "I will make known Your faith with my mouth." Using the mouth (Malkhut) to proclaim God's Malkhut strengthens that realm, and awakens the latent authority needed to overcome all questions and challenges to faith.

Prayer

Malkhut is also expressed through prayer. "Prayer is founded on the belief—the faith—that there exists a Creator Who continually recreates the world as He wishes," Rebbe Nachman explains. "With this belief, you can pray to God that He fulfill your requests. Then, by means of your prayers, you can even effect miracles in the world which defy the laws of nature" (*Likutey Moharan* I, 7:7).

We are used to thinking there is a "natural order" for everything in life. The sun always rises in the east and sets in the west, etc. "That's the way it is; there's nothing anyone can do about it," people say—but they are wrong. True, God created a natural system within which the world operates, but He also brings about "natural" phenomena such as tsunamis, tidal waves, hurricanes, monsoons, volcanoes and earthquakes which, though they have scientific explanations, defy the natural order, showing us that nature can be changed. The Ten Plagues in Egypt, the Splitting of the Sea, and other miracles recorded in the Torah mirror this truth, while in each and every generation many individuals testify to miracles that happened to them.

Prayer gives us the power to defy nature. When we rely on God, Who has the power and authority to do as He pleases, we can invoke that power and effect miracles. Through prayer we become attached to God, the Infinite Source of all our potential, and through prayer we eventually see our goals attained (see *Likutey Moharan* II, 84).

> Accustom yourself to pray for anything you lack, whether livelihood or children or the health of a sick person. In all these things, your primary strategy should be to pray to God. Believe that "God is good for everything" (*Psalms* 145:9)—for healing, for livelihood and for everything else—and the essence of your efforts at obtaining what you need should be directed towards God. Do not chase after other kinds of strategies, since most of them are totally ineffective and we are generally unable to discover even the tiny fraction of them that are effective. But calling to God is good and effective for everything in the world; this method is always available, because God is always there (*Likutey Moharan* I, 14:11).

Prayer is also the most effective tool for surmounting every challenge and obstacle that arises in the course of our lives. "Whatever battles you have to fight—whether against your evil inclination or against those who put barriers and obstacles in your way—should all be fought with prayer," Rebbe Nachman recommends. "Prayer is the source of your very life. Speak to God and beg Him to help you in every way. Prayer is the weapon with which to win the battle" (*Likutey Moharan* I, 2:1).

Admittedly, it's not always easy to pray. Sometimes we're tired, sometimes under pressure, other times angry, or not at peace with ourselves to be able to speak to God. Rebbe Nachman reveals: "The secret of prayer is to be bold. Have the audacity to ask God for everything you need. The only way to stand up and pray to God is with boldness and daring. When you pray, cast aside your timidity and boldly ask God for whatever you need. This boldness is needed to thwart the opposition that tries to prevent you from serving God" (*Likutey Moharan* I, 30). That is, we must take control (i.e., Malkhut) of the situation and, to an extent, "force the issue" of our prayers and requests before God.

> You may sometimes pray with great devotion. But then the feeling departs and the words begin to seem empty. Do not be discouraged. Continue the service, saying each word in absolute simplicity. Sometimes you will try very hard and still not be able to pray. But never become discouraged. This is the most important rule of all. Force yourself to say each word of the service. Make believe that you are a child just learning to read, and simply say the words. In most cases, God will then touch your heart with a flame and it will be aroused to pray with feeling. ...
>
> Listen to every word you say. Concentrate and do not let your thoughts stray. Simply keep your mind on the words of the service. Follow the order of the service even without feeling. Continue word by word, page by page, until God helps you achieve a feeling of devotion. And even if you complete the entire service without feeling, it is not the end. You can still say a psalm. There are other prayers to be said. In general, you must force yourself to do every holy task with all your might. This is especially true of prayer. If you are not worthy, it is still forbidden to become discouraged. Be strong and cheer yourself as much as possible. Pray in happiness, with a joyful tune. Put yourself into a cheerful mood before you begin your worship. Seek out your good points; use them to bring joy to your prayers (*Rabbi Nachman's Wisdom* #75).

Rebbe Nachman was known never to force an issue. Yet when it came to prayer, he insisted upon never being lax. We must exercise our authority—our Malkhut—to be forceful and bold in this area.

Forceful—to make sure we pray and ask for our needs. Bold—because even if we think we may be distant from God—even if we are guilty of terrible sins—nevertheless, we can always approach Him. What we need is the faith that God listens to and hears our prayers. As Rebbe Nachman teaches, "The basis of all prayer is faith—namely, our belief that everything is in God's power, even to alter nature, and that God does not withhold just reward from any creature (*Pesachim* 118; *Likutey Moharan* I, 55:3).

> You may have prayed profusely and secluded yourself with God day after day for years and years, and yet you still feel that you are very far from God. You may even start to think that God is hiding His countenance from you. But it is a mistake for you to think that God does not hear your prayers. Believe with perfect faith that God pays attention to each and every word of all of your prayers, petitions and conversations with Him. Not a single word is lost. Each one leaves its mark in the worlds above, however faintly. Little by little they awaken God's love.

> If there seems to be no response, the reason is that the edifice you are destined to enter is not yet perfected. The main thing is not to give up and fall into despair. That would be foolish. Be firm and continue with your prayers with new determination. In the end, God's love will be aroused and He will turn to you and shine His radiance upon you and fulfill your wishes and desires. He will draw you towards Him in love and abundant mercy (*Likutey Moharan* I, 2:7).

> There are times when you must even conquer God. You may feel that God rejects you because of your sins. You may think that you are still not doing His Will, but remain strong and throw yourself before God. Spread your hands to Him and beg that He have mercy and let you still serve Him. It may seem that God is rejecting you, but cry out, "No matter what! I still want to be close to You!" This is the way you overcome God. God has great joy when you conquer Him this way (*Rabbi Nachman's Wisdom* #69).

Rebbe Nachman says that the main reasons why people do not pray properly are depression and laziness, which both stem from a lack of faith. If their faith were complete and they truly believed God was standing over them and hearing every single word they uttered, they would certainly pray with great fervor and zeal. Similarly, the whole reason that people are far from the Tzaddikim and from true service of God is lack of faith. Nothing stands in the way of one who has complete faith (*Likutey Moharan* I, 155:2).

Prayer refers to the set prayers in the siddur and to spontaneous prayers that arise from the depths of the heart. The latter is referred to in Breslov writings as *hitbodedut*, Rebbe Nachman's unique path of meditation (see below). Both types of prayer are effective in attaining the goal we seek, which is a connection to God. In either case, we can invest our own personalities and desires into our prayers, in the following ways:

> When you pray, be so tightly bound to God that you do not notice anybody else at all. Think that there is nothing in the world except God, and that you yourself are the only creature in the world. All you should hear is what you yourself are saying before God. It is true that the ultimate goal is to surrender yourself so much that you do not even hear yourself. But even if you have not attained this level, you should at least try not to hear anybody else (*Likutey Moharan* II, 103).

> Prayer must be spoken out loud—literally. It is not enough to think the prayers. It is true that God knows what you are thinking. But the words have to be spoken, because speech is a vessel with which you receive the influx of blessing. The blessing you receive is in accordance with the words you speak. When you articulate the words on your lips and your speech is well-ordered and proper, you are able to receive rich blessings. You should pray for whatever you need, whether spiritual or material, in words, and then you will be able to receive the influx of blessing (*Likutey Moharan* I, 34:3).

Hitbodedut

Hitbodedut, Rebbe Nachman's suggested path of meditation, is a type of prayer which is performed in your own language and words. To do hitbodedut, you seclude yourself in a private place such as a quiet room, a park or a field, or any other suitable place where distractions are few or, better yet, nonexistent. During hitbodedut, you talk with God about yourself, your needs and your goals; articulate all your thoughts, questions, frustrations and challenges; and ask God to help you realize your goals. You also express thanks for the things God has given you and the goals you have attained.

Hitbodedut is a powerful tool for conceiving, moving forward and constantly re-evaluating your progress towards your goals. Earlier we spoke of Rebbe Nachman's message that people are not clones and that each person must develop his unique potential (see p. 26). Hitbodedut is the ultimate in original expression, giving you the chance to make direct contact with your Creator and speak out your most personal thoughts and concerns to the Source of all your potential. Hitbodedut represents the pinnacle of recognizing your personality, as you can use this type of meditation to discern your strengths and weaknesses and learn how to make the best use of each of them.

Describing hitbodedut, Rebbe Nachman said, "Make sure to set aside a specific time each day to calmly review your life. Consider what you are doing, and ponder whether it is worthy that you devote your life to it" (Rabbi Nachman's Wisdom #47). The Rebbe himself practiced this. A young man once asked him how to meditate, and the Rebbe told him to say to God: "Master of the World, have pity on me. Is it right that my time should pass in such futility? Was it for this I was created?" Some time later, the young man was standing behind the Rebbe's door and heard him pouring out his heart to God with these very words (Tzaddik #239).

Hitbodedut opens up, supports and strengthens your relationship with God so that you can access the Godly energies hidden in the Sefirot. The more hitbodedut you do, the greater the relationship you will have; the stronger the relationship, the more you will want to engage in hitbodedut. Hitbodedut is crucial to a relationship with God. As a friend of mine once remarked, "How can you have a relationship with someone you never talk to?"

Rebbe Nachman recommends that each person engage in hitbodedut for one hour a day, although less is certainly worthwhile. During this time, gather your thoughts and begin to speak to God, asking Him, pleading with Him, to live as full a life as you possibly can, to accomplish your intended goals, to be focused and keep focused, and to ask for anything you need, such as health and livelihood issues. One who engages in hitbodedut is guaranteed to "taste" God, to experience Him in ways he may have thought were beyond human ability.[21]

> God calls us His children, as it is written (*Deuteronomy* 14:1), "You are children to the Lord your God." Therefore, it is good to express your thoughts and troubles to God, like a child complaining and pestering his father. You may think that you have done so much wrong that you are no longer one of God's children, but remember that God still calls you His child.
>
> Let us assume that God has dismissed you and told you that you are no longer His child. Still, you must say, "Let Him do as He wills. I must do my part and still act like His child." How very good it is when you can awaken your heart and plead until tears stream from your eyes and you stand like a little child crying before his father (*Rabbi Nachman's Wisdom* #7).

Hitbodedut is not only for spiritual gain. Pray for good health, for a good income, and for your emotional needs as well. And pray for all the little things, to connect with all the blessing that God has to bestow on you. Rebbe Nachman suggests:

> Pray for everything. If your garment is torn and must be replaced, pray to God for a new one. Do this for everything. Make it a habit to pray for all your needs, large or small. Your main prayers should be for fundamentals—that God help you in your devotion, that you be worthy of coming close to Him. Still, you should also pray even for trivial things. God may give you food and clothing and everything else you need even though you do not ask for them; but then you

---

[21] For a complete, "how to" guide to hitbodedut, see *Where Earth and Heaven Kiss: A Guide to Rebbe Nachman's Path of Meditation*, published by Breslov Research Institute.

can be compared to an animal. God gives every living thing its bread without being asked. He can also give it to you this way. But if you do not draw your life through prayer, then it is like that of a beast. For a person must draw all of the necessities of life from God only through prayer (*Rabbi Nachman's Wisdom* #233).

Like other kinds of prayer, the words don't always come during hitbodedut. Understand that this is normal and happens more often than we'd like. The Rebbe teaches us never to despair: "When a person is speaking to God in meditation, even if he can say nothing except the words 'Master of the World,' this is also very good" (*Tzaddik* #440). The main thing is to be obstinate and to sit before God, to set aside time to make the connection with Him.

The rewards of hitbodedut are greater than we can imagine:

If you wish to savor the taste of the Hidden Light—the mysteries of Torah, the Kabbalah, the Godly experience, which are destined to be revealed in the Future—you should meditate and speak to God. Express everything in your heart before Him. Examine yourself and judge yourself. Weigh all the different things you are involved with. In this way you will be able to banish your extraneous fears of forces other than God—these are called "fallen fears"—and elevate your fear and experience to the true awe of Heaven (*Likutey Moharan* I, 15:3).

Strive to be totally merged with the Source of your being. To achieve this requires *bitul* (self-nullification), and the only way to attain bitul is through secluded prayer with God (hitbodedut). In this way, you can nullify your corporeality and become merged with your Source (*Likutey Moharan* I, 52). In this way, you ascend beyond the challenges and attain Eternal Life, which is the Ultimate Goal.

Part Four

FROM POTENTIAL
TO ACTUAL

1

THE MAKING OF A TZADDIK

"Sweet is the sleep of the working man ..." *(Ecclesiastes* 5:11).

The Midrash tells a parable about a king who hired workers to tend to his fields. One of the workers put in much more effort than the others. The king pulled him aside and asked him to join him on a stroll through his gardens. Then he sat him down to eat a meal together, and made him his close friend. Seeing this, the other workers demanded, "How come you're favoring him more than us?" The king answered, "He did more for me than anyone else."

The Midrash cites this parable as a eulogy for Rabbi Bun, a leading Talmudic sage who passed away at the young age of twenty-eight. In those twenty-eight years, Rabbi Bun achieved more than the average person could hope to achieve in a lifetime of one hundred years! *(Kohelet Rabbah* 5:11). According to the Midrash, "the sleep of the working man" is sweet because he has struggled to achieve his goals during his lifetime. Then he can "rest" in the afterlife, secure in the rewards from his attainments.

In this vein, Rebbe Nachman once remarked: *"Men darf nisht lang leben, mir darf nohr shein leben!* One does not have to live long, but he should live well!" Rebbe Nachman, too, lived a short life—

he was only thirty-eight years old when he passed away—yet he accomplished more in this brief span of years than most people can hope to achieve in several lifetimes.

Rebbe Nachman began working on himself and perfecting his character traits when he was but a child. He acquired his first disciple on the day of his bar mitzvah, at the age of thirteen. He continued to attract more and more followers, ultimately creating a Chassidut that today numbers in the tens of thousands (not to mention the myriads of interested readers of his works in many languages). Today, nearly two hundred years after his passing, Rebbe Nachman's teachings and parables still possess an astonishing freshness and immediacy that attracts laymen and scholars alike.

His achievement is even more noteworthy considering his background. Rebbe Nachman was a Jewish leader who was active mostly in Eastern Europe in the early nineteenth century. More to the point, he was a Chassidic master, the leader of a very small group of followers during a period when Judaism was being torn asunder by rival Chassidic groups, their outspoken critics in the non-Chassidic world, and the Haskalah (Enlightenment movement), which attempted to divorce Jews from traditional Judaism altogether. How can a Chassidic master of the early nineteenth century speak to people in the twenty-first century, offering with such clarity the advice and wisdom we so desperately need?

The answer, as Rebbe Nachman often said, was that he was not born a Tzaddik. He would always scoff at those who think a Tzaddik is "born that way." Rather, a Tzaddik becomes what he is on the strength of his own efforts. All depends on the individual and how much energy he is willing to invest in his goals and his future (*Rabbi Nachman's Wisdom* #26). True, Rebbe Nachman had good genes (his great-grandfather was the Baal Shem Tov, founder of Chassidism), but he also worked on himself and struggled to achieve greatness using all the tools of the Kabbalah that we have discussed. Using each of the Sefirot, he unlocked the mysteries of Creation and left us a legacy of timeless wisdom.

Here are some examples of how Rebbe Nachman harnessed the energies of the Sefirot to reach his potential:

Keter

When the Rebbe first became involved in his devotions, everything he did required great toil and effort. No form of devotion came easily, and the Rebbe had to literally lay down his life in many cases. Each thing required tremendous effort, and he had to work hard each time he wanted to do something to serve God. He fell *thousands of times* (!), but each time he picked himself up again and served God anew.... Each time he would begin, he would find himself falling. He would then begin anew and stumble yet another time. This occurred countless times, over and over again.... Finally the Rebbe resolved to stand fast and maintain his foothold.... From then on, his heart was firm in its devotion to God (*Rabbi Nachman's Wisdom, His Praises* #5).

Such was Rebbe Nachman's tremendous willpower. He knew the challenges were great, but he remained steadfast in his resolve to accomplish the lofty goals he set for himself. To continually bear the frustrations of trying and stumbling and trying yet again requires a great deal of patience, another aspect of Keter. The Rebbe's efforts towards renewal (conceptually, the idea of repentance) gave him the energy to shrug off each setback and dig in for another fresh start. In his later years he said, "That a single word does not leave my lips without some innovation—that goes without saying. Not even a breath leaves my lips without originality!" (*Tzaddik* #384).

Chokhmah, Binah, Daat

In the very first lesson of *Likutey Moharan*, Rebbe Nachman teaches that a person must use his mind to find God in literally everything in this world.

Rebbe Nachman constantly used his mind to investigate and analyze everything he could to better his life. Throughout his teachings, we find references not only to the Torah insights that were so dear to him, but also to all sorts of ideas about natural phenomena. The latter include references to the human anatomy, animal behavior and the vegetable and mineral kingdoms. Perhaps the most amazing of these discussions centers on human behavior, predating modern psychology by one hundred years!

Not only was the Rebbe able to understand the difficulties facing each and every person in this world, but he never shied away from offering down-to-earth solutions for each person's survival and growth. His advice works equally for the shtetl Jew in nineteenth-century Ukraine and the cosmopolitan Jew in twenty-first century New York because he looked for God in everything. Rebbe Nachman knew that God conceived the individual or collective problem—and God also provides the solution. Anyone who seeks the Source and Goal of this world will be rewarded with understanding.

Chesed

Rebbe Nachman once remarked: "The love between the Tzaddik and his followers is true love, the very essence of love. The Tzaddik's love for his followers is very, very great: he desires their true good. If he could, he would give them all the good of all the worlds…and he would wish them to have beautifully decorated homes, gardens and so on.…How much more does he want their *spiritual* good" (*Tzaddik* #471).

"I have put everything aside and given myself over to you, so as to make you better people," the Rebbe told his followers. "This is more important than everything else.…How many times have I become hoarse and dry in the mouth from talking and talking with each one of you! And what have I achieved? You may be pure and sincere, but that isn't what I wanted. I wanted you to be Tzaddikim—outstanding Tzaddikim on the highest of levels" (*Tzaddik* #257).

Filling his heart with love and concern, Rebbe Nachman spent much time and effort thinking about and helping others. He once said that every one of his followers was "baked in his heart." He wanted only the best for them, both physically and spiritually, and exhorted them to always try their best, never to remain satisfied with second-class achievements. "Don't settle for less," the Rebbe would say. "Never give up. You *can* do better."

The Rebbe was with his followers in sorrow as in joy. He made himself feel the suffering of each petitioner, whether it be the ravages of illness, the heartbreak of childlessness or the despair of poverty. Rebbe Nachman said that God helped him to feel others' pain even more than they did (*Rabbi Nachman's Wisdom* #188).

Gevurah

One must be very stubborn when serving God (*Likutey Moharan* II, 48).

Gevurah calls for strength and resolve as well as the willingness to give up one's preconceived notions, creature comforts and, sometimes, one's very self. Rebbe Nachman harnessed this energy when he undertook a pilgrimage to the Land of Israel in 1798-1799. He lacked proper funding, had to leave his wife and children for the duration, and even gave up his standing as a Chassidic master prior to his departure. He set aside all these concerns in favor of the spiritual imperative of establishing his physical presence in the Holy Land. Moreover, he summoned incredible self-control to remain focused on his goal for the five long months it took him to complete the perilous journey by land and sea from Ukraine to the port of Haifa—where he said he was finally able to grasp *Chokhmah Ila'ah* (Divine Perceptions of Wisdom).

Tiferet

When he first began to serve God, Rebbe Nachman would choose certain devotions that, after deep consideration, he felt were proper for him to do at that time. After he made his decision, he would embark on that path and stay with it, never letting any recurring doubts about the efficacy of those devotions disturb him.

After several weeks had passed, he would review his path, and either continue with his chosen devotions or choose others (*Likutey Moharan* II, 115).

Whether a devotion proved effective or had to be discarded, Rebbe Nachman was always at peace with himself. He would pick up on the things that presented themselves to him at the moment and use them to the best of his ability. When the results came in, he would reassess his choices and make new ones. In the end, his gains offset his losses.

The Rebbe also invested every available moment, from a very young age, to amass Torah knowledge. With this knowledge he could base all his choices on sound and enduring principles. As a young child, he would pay his tutor three silver coins from his own pocket money for each page of Talmud that he was taught. This was in addition to the regular tuition paid by his father. The Rebbe would add his own bonus for each page so his tutor would exert himself to teach him many pages each day (*Rabbi Nachman's Wisdom, His Praises* #4).

Reb Noson relates: "The Rebbe devoted every available moment to his sacred studies. He spent much time studying the Talmud, the Shulchan Arukh, the Torah, the Ein Yaakov[22] and the mystical books of the Zohar, Tikkuney Zohar and the writings of the holy ARI. The Rebbe said that his father's library contained all the small Mussar books, and that he went through every one....He was fluent in the entire Torah. He could quote anything in the sacred literature as if the book was opened in front of him. It was like a table set before him, where he could see everything and choose what he desired. The entire scope of our sacred literature was like this, standing ready before his mind's eye to be used whenever he desired. This can be seen to some extent in the Rebbe's writings" (*Rabbi Nachman's Wisdom, His Praises* #7).

---

22 "The Well of Jacob," a compilation of all the portions of the Talmud not dealing with legal questions.

Netzach, Hod

Rebbe Nachman told Reb Noson: "Whatever I have to accomplish, I always want to do it and finish it immediately without delay, without leaving it for another time. If it had been possible to complete the writing of the *Sefer HaMidot* (The Aleph-Bet Book) in a single day, I would have gladly done it" (Tzaddik #434).

Knowing when to move forward and when to hold back—this was the genius Rebbe Nachman applied to all his activities. He never stood still; rather, he did whatever needed to be done without delay. He knew that if he didn't do it immediately, he might never get around to doing it, because later on he would not want to have to think about it at all. However, if he could not do something immediately, he would never become agitated. If he could do it later—the next day or some other time—he would do it; and if not, then not. He was never in the least bit tense or agitated about anything (ibid.).

Yesod

The Rebbe said: "To me, men and women are alike" (Rabbi Nachman's Wisdom, His Praises #18).

Reb Noson explains that Rebbe Nachman attained such a lofty degree of morality that he was able to completely break any lustful thoughts or feelings he might have. Afterwards, he never had any wayward thoughts when looking at a woman. As explained earlier, this attainment of purity accords the person the title of Tzaddik (see p. 134).

"Do not think that such self-control was a simple matter," Reb Noson notes. "In order to gain total control over his sexual instincts, the Rebbe had to battle countless temptations. It required many days and years of praying and begging and pouring out his heart before God, pleading that He rescue him from this desire. The Rebbe continued along this path until he was able to withstand all temptation. He sanctified himself to such a degree that his total separation from this desire cannot be imagined. In the end, he was worthy of totally subjugating it. He worked on himself until he actually found it difficult to understand how people could consider lust difficult to control. For to him, it was no longer any temptation at all" (*Rabbi Nachman's Wisdom, His Praises* #16).

With similar determination, Rebbe Nachman conquered each of his negative character traits. "At first he was very bad-tempered, becoming angry at the slightest provocation. But still, he wanted to be a good, kind person, as God desires. He began working on his temper until he overcame it completely. He rejected anger totally, pushing himself to the opposite extreme. In the place of anger, he now had absolute patience and tolerance. He reached a stage where nothing bothered him at all.... No matter how much bad a person did to him, he would tolerate it without any hatred whatsoever" (*Rabbi Nachman's Wisdom, His Praises* #22).

Malkhut

The main way the Rebbe attained what he did was simply through prayer and supplication before God. He was very consistent in this. He would beg and plead in every way possible, asking that God have mercy and make him worthy of true devotion and closeness (*Rabbi Nachman's Wisdom, His Praises* #10).

Speaking in his own language (Yiddish), Rebbe Nachman would seclude himself in the same place each day to express his thoughts to God. His father's house contained a small garret that was partitioned off as a storehouse for hay and feed. There he sequestered himself to recite psalms and pray.

"He also made use of every published prayer he could find, and recited them countless times," Reb Noson recalls. "He poured out his heart in every possible prayer and supplication, even those printed in Yiddish for women. Not a single one was omitted.... He also had the practice of reciting only the verses in the psalms speaking of prayer and the cry to God. He would go through the entire Book of Psalms in one stretch, saying only those verses and leaving out the rest.

"But beyond all this, the main thing was his own prayers, emanating from his heart in his own language. He would pray and argue before God, making up petitions and arguments as he went along. He would beg and plead that God make him worthy of true devotion. It was prayers such as these that helped Rebbe Nachman achieve his greatness. We heard this explicitly from the Rebbe's own holy lips" (ibid.).

Faith is a necessary companion to prayer. Rebbe Nachman used to say, "It is very good to rely on God completely. As each day begins, I place my every movement in God's hands, asking that I do only His Will. This is very good, and I have no worries. Whether or not things go right, I am completely dependent on God. If He desires otherwise, I have already asked that I do only His Will. Before each Shabbat or festival, I also place my observance in God's hands, asking that it all be according to His Will. I can then celebrate without worrying that I am doing something wrong, since I am completely dependent on God!" (Rabbi Nachman's Wisdom #2).

Rebbe Nachman also displayed faith in Tzaddikim from an early age. When he was no more than six years old, he would walk from his home in Medziboz to the nearby grave of his holy great-grandfather, the Baal Shem Tov, and ask that Tzaddik to help him draw close to God. Afterwards he would immerse in a mikvah. He would do this at night, even during the winter frosts, so that no one would see him (Rabbi Nachman's Wisdom, His Praises #19).

2

❧

FULL CIRCLE

The stage is set; the world is ready to be created. Having filtered down through each of the Ten Sefirot, God's Light is released into our world, illuminating all of Creation with blessing and bounty. Now it is up to us to return blessing and bounty to God through our performance of mitzvot and recognition of God's Sovereignty over the world. In this way we fulfill the purpose of Creation and attain the Ultimate Goal.

The stage is also set for each one of us. We are ready to create our own worlds and fill them with physical and spiritual blessings. To achieve our goals, we need the Ten Sefirot to direct and channel our energies. By cultivating and perfecting the various attributes represented by the Sefirot, we can turn our potential into actuality.

As Rebbe Nachman teaches, the main thrust of this creation process relates to the attainment of spiritual goals. We can spend seventy, eighty, even one hundred years in this physical world, but our existence in the World to Come will last for eternity. Therefore the Rebbe applies the lessons of the Kabbalah to achieving long-term goals, like the wonderful Future that awaits us in the World to Come.

Nonetheless, these strategies can also be applied to any area of life. For example, the energies of the Sefirot can be used to develop emotional stability. One who has faith gains the courage of his convictions and the ability to stand up under pressure. The greater his faith, the greater his ability to believe in himself and deal with his daily challenges.

The same is true of physical and financial soundness. Not everyone has excellent health, nor does everyone attain financial success. These depend on God's Will, and are God's means of testing our ability to accomplish even when saddled by setbacks. But if we focus on and use the attributes and energies we do possess, we are in a better position to cope with difficulties in a positive manner and discover new avenues for achievement.

The main requirement for establishing goals and then attaining them is willpower. All desire is rooted in Keter (will), which receives its energy directly from God. If we prepare our vessels accordingly, we can receive and channel that energy in accordance with our abilities.

We must recall that our ultimate objective is to attain recognition of God, the Source of our potential. After the energy of Keter has filtered down to us through the Sefirot, we redirect that light and energy back to God. Coming full circle, we connect ourselves with God, the Limitless Source of all energy and potential, and are ready for the next step: to ascend to greater levels and ever greater achievements. Our guideposts are the writings of the Kabbalists and the teachings of Tzaddikim of all generations, whose directives steer us through the maze of challenges so that we can develop our potential to the highest level possible.

Reb Noson writes that the key to actualizing our potential is an unquenchable yearning for God, Who is both the Source and the Goal. The more we increase our desire to connect with God, the greater the energy of the Keter—God's Will—we can draw out. With this awesome energy burning within us, we have the power to counter any temptation or material lust that occludes our focus, and ascend beyond all obstacles to fulfill our goals.

For this reason we find that the Hebrew word for will is *RatZon*, which is etymologically similar to *RatZ* (run). One who has a burning desire will "run" the course of life with great enthusiasm, always pursuing his will, his goal *(Likutey Halakhot, Birkat HaRei'ach 5:5)*.

* * *

May God help us to recognize the awesome potential for good that we all have within us, and let us develop it to the point that we merit to reach our goals on all levels—physical, financial, emotional and spiritual. Through this unity of energies we will also attain inner peace and harmony with the world around us, which leads to the Ultimate Goal of Creation—the Comprehensive Peace that will reign in the Days of the Mashiach (see *Isaiah* 11:6-9). By reaching our own goals, we can bring the entire world to peace!

May peace, the culmination of unity, reign throughout the world. Amen.

Appendix

THE ORDER OF THE TEN SEFIROT

כתר
KETER

חכמה
CHOKHMAH

בינה
BINAH

חסד
CHESED

גבורה
GEVURAH

תפארת
TIFERET

נצח
NETZACH

הוד
HOD

יסוד
YESOD

מלכות
MALKHUT

THE STRUCTURE OF THE SEFIROT

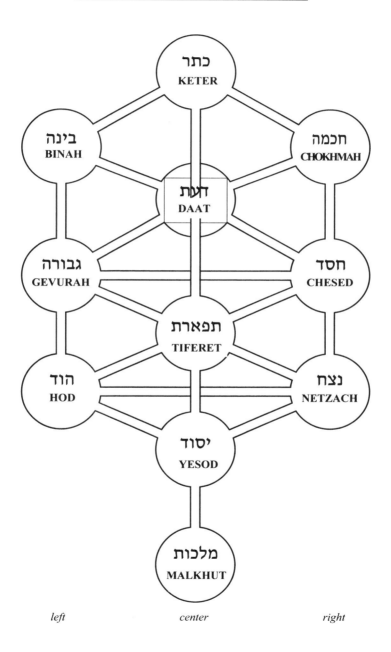

left　　　　　　*center*　　　　　　*right*

THE PARTZUFIM - THE DIVINE PERSONAS

Sefirah		Persona
KETER		ATIK YOMIN
		ARIKH ANPIN
CHOKHMAH		ABBA
	Daat	
BINAH		IMMA
	Chesed	
	Gevurah	
	Tiferet	
TIFERET	Netzach	ZEIR ANPIN
	Hod	
	Yesod	
MALKHUT		NUKVA of ZEIR ANPIN

Alternative names for *Zeir Anpin* and *Malkhut*:

Zeir Anpin: Yaakov, Yisrael, Yisrael Sava, Torah, Written Law, Holy King, the Sun.
Malkhut: Leah, Rachel, Prayer, Oral Law, *Shekhinah* (Divine Presence), the Moon.

THE SEFIROT AND MAN

Keter - Crown, Will	Skull
Chokhmah - Wisdom	Right brain
Binah - Understanding	Left brain
(*Daat* - Knowledge, Awareness)	(Middle brain)
Chesed - Lovingkindness	Right arm
Gevurah - Strength, Restraint	Left Arm
Tiferet - Beauty, Harmony	Torso
Netzach - Victory, Endurance	Right leg
Hod - Splendor	Left leg
Yesod - Foundation	Sexual organ (*Brit*)
Malkhut - Kingship	Feet

Alternatively: *Chokhmah* corresponds to brain/mind; *Binah* to heart
Alternatively: *Malkhut* corresponds to man's mate, or the mouth

LEVELS OF EXISTENCE

World	Manifestation	Sefirah	Soul	Letter
Adam Kadmon		*Keter*	*Yechidah*	*Apex of Yod*
Atzilut	Nothingness	*Chokhmah*	*Chayah*	*Yod*
Beriyah	Thought	*Binah*	*Neshamah*	*Heh*
Yetzirah	Speech	*Tiferet* (six *sefirot*)	*Ruach*	*Vav*
Asiyah	Action	*Malkhut*	*Nefesh*	*Heh*

World	Inhabitants	T-N-T-A
Adam Kadmon	The Holy Names	
Atzilut - Nearness	Sefirot, Partzufim	*Taamim* -Cantillations
Beriyah - Creation	The Throne, Souls	*Nekudot* - Vowels
Yetzirah - Formation	Angels	*Tagim* - Crowns
Asiyah - Action	Forms	*Otiyot* - Letters

THE SUPERNAL COLORS

Keter - Crown, Will	blinding invisible white
Chokhmah - Wisdom	a color that includes all color
Binah - Understanding	yellow and green
Chesed - Lovingkindness	white and silver
Gevurah - Strength, Restraint	red and gold
Tiferet - Beauty, Harmony	yellow and purple
Netzach - Victory, Endurance	light pink
Hod - Splendor	dark pink
Yesod - Foundation	orange
Malkhut - Kingdom	blue

THE SEVEN SUPERNAL SHEPHERDS

Chesed - Lovingkindness	Avraham
Gevurah - Strength, Restraint	Yitzchak
Tiferet - Beauty, Harmony	Yaakov
Netzach - Victory, Endurance	Moshe
Hod - Splendor	Aharon
Yesod - Foundation	Yosef
Malkhut - Kingdom	David

HEBREW/ENGLISH TRANSLITERATION SCHEMA

lamed	L	ל	aleph, alef	silent*	א
mem	M	מ, ם	bet, beit	B	ב
nun	N	נ, ן	vet	V	ב
samakh	S	ס	gimel	G	ג
ayin	silent*	ע	dalet	D	ד
peh	P	פ	heh	H	ה
pheh	Ph, F	פ, ף	vav	V, O, U	ו, וֹ, וּ
tzadi	TZ	צ, ץ	zayin	Z	ז
kuf, kuph	K	ק	chet	Ch	ח
reish	R	ר	tet	T	ט
shin	Sh	שׁ	yod, yud	Y	י
sin	S	שׂ	kaf, kaph	K	כ
tav	T	ת	khaf, khaph	Kh	כ, ך

* the letters א and ע are "silent" consonants (with no English letter-equivalents) and are transliterated based on their accompanying vowel point, as either A, Æ E, I, Œ or U

HEBREW LETTER NUMEROLOGY - GEMATRIA

300 = ש	70 = ע	20 = כ, ך	6 = ו	1 = א
400 = ת	80 = פ, ף	30 = ל	7 = ז	2 = ב
	90 = צ, ץ	40 = מ, ם	8 = ח	3 = ג
	100 = ק	50 = נ, ן	9 = ט	4 = ד
	200 = ר	60 = ס	10 = י	5 = ה

alternate values for the 5 end-letters, *MaNTzPaKh:*

900 = ץ   800 = ף   700 = ן   600 = ם   500 = ך

Glossary

ARI—an acronym for Rabbi Yitzchak Luria (1534-1572), Jewish scholar and founder of the modern study of the Kabbalah

Baal Shem Tov—lit., "Master of the Good Name," the appellation for Rabbi Yisrael ben Eliezer (1700-1760), founder of Chassidut and great-grandfather of Rebbe Nachman of Breslov

Bitul—negation, nullification. In a mystical context, refers to total nullification of the ego.

Brit—covenant

Brit Milah—covenant of circumcision

Chassidut—a Jewish revival movement founded in Eastern Europe in the eighteenth century by Rabbi Yisrael ben Eliezer, the Baal Shem Tov. One of its core teachings is that God's presence fills all one's surroundings, and one should strive to serve God in every word and deed.

Gehinnom—Hell

Haggadah—liturgy of the Pesach Seder

Halakhah—Jewish law

Hitbodedut—lit., "self-seclusion," a form of prayer and verbal meditation. Rebbe Nachman uses the term to refer to a daily practice in which one sets aside a time and place to speak to God.

Kabbalah—body of mystical Jewish wisdom

Kav—ray or line

Kiddush—lit., "sanctification," the ceremony of reciting blessings over wine at the onset of Shabbat and festival meals

Mashiach—the Jewish Messiah, descendant of King David

Matzah—unleavened bread eaten on Pesach

Midot—Characteristics or Attributes; another name for the seven lower Sefirot of Chesed, Gevurah, Tiferet, Netzach, Hod, Yesod and Malkhut

Mikvah—a special pool of water used for ritual purification

Mitzvah (pl. *mitzvot*)—Torah precept or commandment

Mochin—Intellects; another name for the upper Sefirot of Chokhmah, Binah and Daat.

Mussar—ethical lessons for personal and spiritual growth

Ohr Ein Sof—God's Infinite Light

Pesach—the Jewish Passover, a biblical festival commemorating the Exodus from Egypt, occurring in spring

Seder—lit., "order," the festival meal conducted on the first two nights of Passover (on the first night only in the Land of Israel), with a prescribed order of rituals and symbolic foods that recall the Exodus from Egypt

Sefirah (pl. *Sefirot*)—Divine interfaces through which God's blessings come down to man, and man sends his personal offerings up to God

Shabbat—the Jewish Sabbath

Shavuot—biblical festival commemorating the Giving of the Torah at Mount Sinai, occurring in late spring

Shma, Shma Yisrael—a declaration of faith in the oneness of God and a commitment to fulfilling His commandments, comprised of verses from *Deuteronomy* 6:4-9 and 11:13-21 and *Numbers* 15:37-41. Recited daily during morning and evening prayers, and before going to sleep.

Shmirat HaBrit—guarding the covenant. Specifically refers to the rite of circumcision and conceptually, to maintaining sexual purity.

Shulchan Arukh—the Code of Jewish Law, compiled by Rabbi Yosef Caro (1488-1575), the benchmark of Halakhah for all Jews

Siddur—Jewish prayer book

Sukkot—biblical festival commemorating God's benevolent care of the Jewish People during their forty-year sojourn in the desert and His continuing Providence over material blessing, occurring in autumn

Talmud—the Jewish Oral Tradition, expounded by the rabbinical leaders between approximately 50 B.C.E. and 500 C.E. The first part of the Talmud, called the Mishnah, was codified by Rabbi Yehudah HaNasi around 188 C.E. The second part, called the Gemara, was edited by Rav Ashi and Ravina around 505 C.E.

Tikkun—rectification

Tikkun HaKlali—Rebbe Nachman's "General Remedy," the recital of Ten Psalms that rectify sins (especially sexual transgressions) at their source

Tzaddik (pl. *Tzaddikim*)—righteous person; one who has spiritually perfected himself

Tzimtzum—constriction or challenge; when capitalized, refers to God's initial contraction of His Infinite Light in order to create our world

Zohar— the greatest classic of the Kabbalah, a mystical commentary on the Torah authored by Rabbi Shimon bar Yochai in the second century C.E.